# FROM
# Raindrops
## TO AN ocean

# KASHYAP PATEL, MD
## & MAHARSHI PATEL

# FROM
# Raindrops
## TO AN ocean

## An Indian–American Oncologist
## Discovers Faith's Power From A Patient

## AMBASSADOR INTERNATIONAL
### GREENVILLE, SOUTH CAROLINA & BELFAST, NORTHERN IRELAND

www.ambassador-international.com

# FROM RAINDROPS TO AN OCEAN
*An Indian-American Oncologist Discovers Faith's Power From A Patient*

© 2012 by Kashyap Patel, MD

Printed in the United States of America

ISBN: 9781935507833

Cover Design & Page Layout by David Siglin

AMBASSADOR INTERNATIONAL
Emerald House
427 Wade Hampton Blvd.
Greenville, SC 29609, USA
www.ambassador-international.com

AMBASSADOR BOOKS
The Mount
2 Woodstock Link
Belfast, BT6 8DD, Northern Ireland, UK
www.ambassador-international.com

*The colophon is a trademark of Ambassador*

# DEDICATION

WITHOUT THE HELP, GUIDANCE AND friendship of a number of people, this book would not have come to fruition. I first want to thank Shelton Sanford, Connie McIntyre, and their family for their candid and frank recollections as they shared every minute detail of their personal lives and memories of Anne Sanford. I want to thank my family, especially my dear wife Alpa, my son Maharshi, and my parents Premila and Bhogi, for their constant inspiration and putting up with the frustrations that arose from the process of my writing. I also want to thank my business partners Dr. Welsh, Dr. Gor, Dr. Naidu, and Dr. Nathwani for allowing me to be more flexible with my time during the writing process. I also want to thank Becky Turner for guiding me through the writing process. I also want to thank my dear friends Swati and Vijay Daji for their constant support. Finally, I want to thank the late Anne Sanford for watching over me and inspiring me as I try to share her story.

From *Raindrops to An Ocean* is a remarkable story of Anne Sanford, a women who even in her darkest days never lost faith in God. Her spirit was one of grace and dignity. She touched all that knew her. Her deep spiritual life is beautifully felt and revealed by Dr. Patel.
—**Mary Brantley**

"In his inspiring book, *From Raindrops to An Ocean*, Dr. Kashyap Patel tells the story of Anne Sanford, a woman whose deeply held spiritual beliefs and practices sustained and delivered her through a challenging ordeal with leukemia that ended in her death.

Because of its focus on the core human experiences of mortality, impermanence, and questions about meaning and purpose, this book will speak to a variety of readers facing serious challenges in their lives, including those not facing life-threatening illness. Dr. Patel's account of Anne Sanford's story should also appeal to spiritual seekers regardless of faith tradition."
—**Jeffrey G Brantley**

# TABLE OF

# CONTENTS

# FOREWORD

THROUGHOUT HUMAN HISTORY, PHILOSOPHERS AND theologians, the educated and the uneducated, the rich and the poor have searched for meaning in human suffering. Suffering is no respecter of persons. We live in a fallen world in which suffering is common to all mankind.

The providence of God is one of the most remarkable and comforting beliefs of the Christian faith. The providence of God means that God is in control and that God is in charge.

Human history is under the control of the sovereign hand of God. In fact, human history is His story. At times our lives may seem so small and insignificant, but when seen in light of the greater story of God, they become extremely valuable and highly significant.

This book is about the story of Anne Sanford, who was my childhood sweetheart and beloved wife of 37 years. In the providence of God, she was called to suffer with an aggressive form of leukemia. She was diagnosed with AML on February 14, 2005, and went home to be with the Lord on March 7, 2006.

Upon Anne's diagnosis, her greatest desire was to be a faithful witness to her Lord and Savior Jesus Christ. Anne's witness has continued long after her death as is evident by the content of this book.

Her faithful witness touched many people's lives and has been an encouragement to those who are going through times of suffering, especially with the terrible disease of cancer.

The providence of God involves both circumstances and people. In God's providence, He brought Dr. Kashyap Patel into the lives of the members of my family.

Kashyap is one of the most caring and compassionate people that I have ever met as well as an exceptional oncologist. His philosophy of medicine includes a combination of the most advanced medical knowledge and technology, the recognition of the importance of the spiritual dynamics of life, and the great value of relationships with family and friends.

As a pastor with over 30 years of ministry experience, I have come to appreciate Kashyap's approach to medicine. Kashyap and I deeply value the importance of the spiritual dimension of life toward the overall health of an individual. We do, however, differ on our faith views. Kashyap has been greatly influenced by his Hindu and Buddhist roots in India as well as various forms of Christianity. Our family, on the other hand, has embraced evangelical Christianity from a reformed and Presbyterian perspective. This book is not an apologetic work defending either of our faith views. However, you will note our distinctive views throughout the book.

This book is the story of a Godly woman who faced suffering with dignity and faith. Anne's story is one of encouragement and hope in the midst of difficult sufferings. She finished her earthly life fulfilling her greatest desire to be a faithful witness of Jesus Christ. At Anne's memorial service, the testimony of her life was compared to the testimony of the apostle Paul's life in II Timothy 4:7-8.

"I have fought the good fight, I have finished the race, I have kept the faith. Henceforth, there is laid up for me the crown of righteousness, which the Lord, the righteous judge, will award to me on that day, and not only to me but to all who have loved his appearing."

Hopefully, our story, as told by Kashyap, will be a great encouragement to you. Even through our difficult times of suffering, we can have hope and experience God's peace.

**—Dr. Shelton P. Sanford**
Senior Pastor
Westminister Presbyterian Church
Rock Hill, SC

# CHAPTER I

# GATHERING CLOUDS

*Though life's goodness can at times be momentarily overshadowed, it can never be outweighed. For every single act of senseless destruction, there are thousands more acts of caring and compassion. For every single thing that causes dismay, there are far more reasons for hope. Don't be satisfied to simply count your many blessings. Live them fully. Consider all the possibilities that life's goodness affords you. Choose to live the best of them with love, vigor, and commitment. Wrap your thoughts, your actions, yourself around life's enduring goodness, and give your best to it. Make it grow ever stronger, and you will too.*
—RALPH MARSTON

ANNE SANFORD AND HER HUSBAND, Pastor Shelton Sanford, were two of those rare few in the world who had always devoted their lives for the good of others. The pastorate is often illustrated as shepherds who watch over a flock of followers; they provide comfort and aid to the suffering, regardless of the cost to themselves. They are the symbol of protection and are looked to for wisdom and help. Pastor Sanford and Anne went above and beyond the usual calling of the profession and together served as a beacon of hope for thousands of people. Nevertheless, at times this world demands that pain enter the households of even those who have devoted their entire lives to dealing with the pain that touches others. With that thought in mind, the story of Anne begins.

My entrance into Anne's life began on one of those winter afternoons that everyone wishes to forget. The sun had not been seen for a week, and the clouds cast dark, gloomy shadows on everything they touched. The trees outside my office window were threadbare, and the fountain that was so soothing only a few short weeks ago to the patients receiving chemo had long since frozen over. You see, I am a doctor of oncology; I specialize in the diagnosis and treatment of cancer. I was determined to end the day as soon as possible. My son was going back to college the next morning and was distinctly displeased that I had rarely been home during his break, so I had promised him coffee and some one-on-one time that afternoon. My paperwork was finished, and I was exhausted after a particularly trying day. Sadly enough, I had to counsel two terminally ill patients that medicine could no longer prolong their lives and that all I could do was try to make them as comfortable as possible in their last few months on earth. That is without a doubt the most difficult aspect of my job. Seeing a person's hopes and dreams crumble before my very eyes never gets any easier, despite having witnessed it countless times before. Inevitably after such a conversation, I always have to retire to my office to regain my composure and wipe a furtive tear from my eye.

I made it as far as the door when my intercom rang. The receptionist asked if I was free to speak with Dr. Truesdale from Shiland Family Practice. The name was not familiar—apparently I had never met nor spoken with her before. My frustrated grimace indicated my displeasure. I responded by asking if Dr. Truesdale could call back on Monday. Much to my dismay, Dr. Truesdale asked to speak to me as soon as possible. With a sigh of resignation, I told the receptionist to put the family practice doctor through.

"Hi, Dr. Patel," she said. "I know we have never met, and I'm really sorry to be bothering you like this. Your receptionist said you were on your way out, but I was hoping to reach you before your weekend began. Your reputation in the field of oncology has led me to call with a special request. One of my patients, a very kind lady named Anne Sanford, has developed bruising over her legs, and her platelets are also low. Would you mind looking at her today and determining what's going on there?"

While I was undoubtedly flattered, I was a bit annoyed that my apparently well- known reputation as an oncologist would cause my lesser-known but equally important reputation as a father to suffer. I did know, however, that despite my son's frustration over my reneging on a promise to him, he would understand that with the line of work I chose, patients need much time and care. Cancer isn't a disease I can prescribe a drug for and then be done with. Treating it includes a holistic approach along with frank and candid discussions, often lasting hours, with the patient and family members concerning the potential of death and how to embrace what comes. To ensure that each patient receives the time they need, I refuse to wear a watch to the office. It often results in patients having to wait while I finish with others, but not a single one ever complains. My son understands this. For that reason alone, he wouldn't be upset that I had to stay.

"Please send Mrs. Sanford my way," I replied to Dr. Truesdale. "It's been a pleasure talking with you. I'll be sure to drop by your office one of these days to put a face with the name."

Anne arrived within a half hour. I would later realize just how much of an understatement Dr. Truesdale had made when she described Anne as a very kind lady, for after our initial interactions, Anne proved to be one of the most pleasant individuals to ever walk through the doors of my clinic. She was accompanied by her daughter Connie, an ER nurse I had met several times before. I immediately remembered Connie for her pleasantness and ease of cooperation--traits that are typically very lacking in interactions between private physicians and ER staff.

The instant I opened the door to the exam room and set eyes on her, I noticed that Anne had something special within her. She radiated a brilliant halo of welcome and comfort about her, one that emanated warmth and made what was usually a very stressful conversation much easier. In my line of work, I am naturally the one who has to put the patient at ease. With Anne, the exact opposite was happening; she was easing any apprehensions that I had before beginning our conversation.

I smiled and said, "Hello, Mrs. Sanford and Mrs. McIntyre, I'm Dr. Patel. Dr. Truesdale called me a little while ago to let me know you would be coming in. Tell me, what can I do for you today?"

Connie replied, "Thank you for seeing us, Dr. Patel. My mom's feeling very weak and tired. She also aches all over, almost as if she has a bad case of the flu. She was running a low-grade fever until yesterday. This morning, she noticed a bruise and some tiny red spots along her legs. During our visit earlier today, Dr. Truesdale checked her blood count and said that my mom's platelets were very low. That's why we're here." She paused for a second and then added, "By the way, I've seen you in the ER a number of times. I've always admired your bedside manner. Your patients seem to love and adore the way you take care of them. We were relieved that you could see Mom so soon."

As I turned towards Anne I thought she actually looked very familiar. Every so often in life, we come across a person whose face seems to remain with us, always looking strangely yet reassuringly and pleasantly familiar. Anne's was one of those faces. Suddenly I realized where I had seen her before. Anne was a volunteer at

Piedmont Medical Center where I did my rounds. Her face was the first one I would see behind the information desk at the surgery center when I walked in the main entrance every morning. I distinctly recalled her face had a perennial smile that brought joy and raised the spirits of everyone who saw her. I also remembered that she had once helped my son when he was hopelessly lost in the maze of hallways in the hospital on the first day of his internship there.

"Oh, Mrs. Sanford, I remember you! I've seen you about two or three times a week for the past year now. You may even recall helping my son find his way when he had been lost and wandering around the hospital for almost forty-five minutes!"

Anne laughed, and the sound floated like musical notes on the air. "Please, you don't have to be formal with me. You can call me Anne. And of course I remember your son Maharshi. He mentioned while we were talking that his father was an oncologist there. By the way, you have one of the most handsome boys I've ever seen!" She then added, "I don't think I have anything serious happening to me. It's just a little cold and some aches. I didn't take the precaution of a flu vaccine this year. Connie is a bit more concerned than I am."

"Well then," I replied, "let's just take a look to be sure. Allow me to run a few tests, and then we'll know for sure what's going on."

I immediately knew what had concerned Connie. As an ER nurse, she was well versed with the symptoms of leukemia: the easy bruising, the painful aches, the nagging low fever, and above all, the low platelet count. She didn't have to mention it by name; the look on her face was enough for me to know that my guess about her concern was correct. My first instinct, however, was in support of Anne's theory. Chances were that her symptoms were most attributable to a simple case of the flu.

Anne looked pale and somewhat feverish. She had light pink spots on both her feet up to her ankles. She also had a large bruise over the back of her left leg. I was fairly certain that it would turn out to be nothing more serious than a viral infection. And yet, in my profession, I have learned that a situation is almost never what it seems at first glance. For that reason, before I offered any encouragement either way, I asked a nurse to draw some of Anne's blood so that I could analyze it and decide on a next step.

After Anne left, I examined her blood under the microscope and was very glad that I hesitated about offering premature reassurances. I saw a preponderance of large, immature, and angry-looking cells. I still leaned on the side of wishful thinking, however, and contemplated that the large abnormal cells could be a result of a lack of Vitamin B12, which causes megaloblastic anemia. I called her in again to go over my findings. She returned with her spirit still as lively as ever. Even as I became more guarded and watchful while explaining to her that I would have to schedule a bone marrow biopsy, her upbeat nature remained unbowed.

She simply asked, "Dr. Patel, I'm ready for the test, but could you explain exactly what it is?"

"Sure, Anne, I don't mind explaining. Think of your bone marrow as a factory. It manufactures all of your blood cells. Now, what we need to do is check to see if your cells are being manufactured properly. Looking at the precursor stem cells in your bone marrow will allow me to determine that. First, I'm going to give you a shot that will freeze the right side of your hipbone so that you will not experience too much discomfort. I'll then have to insert a small-bore needle to aspirate a drop of blood from your bone marrow cavity. After that, I'll make a small cut to insert a larger needle into the same hole. Lastly, I will remove a small core of bone that will be examined underneath a microscope. I know it sounds painful, but thanks to the novocaine that will be used to freeze your hipbone, you won't feel any pain at all after the prick of the first injection," I explained.

"Well, in that case, let's be done with it!" she replied. We scheduled an appointment for the next day. While Connie understood the implications of what the test results could bring, Shelton, Anne's husband, was totally unaware. He was getting ready to go to Taiwan for his next international board meeting and wanted Anne well so that she could go with him.

Anne Sanford was indeed a fighter, and the possibility of leukemia seemed to bother her less than the fact that she was feeling weak and tired. She would be unable to fully devote herself to the many volunteer activities at the church and hospital if she continued to feel this poorly. Anne had always wanted to live her life to the fullest possible extent, at any cost. She had been very active her whole life and did not hesitate to embrace the "big steps" of life's challenges.

Born to a prominent family in Macon, Georgia, Anne Burns Sanford grew up with the privilege of the proverbial silver spoon. After marrying, life continued to be good until Shelton experienced some business losses. Regardless of the ups and downs of running a business, Shelton had been sensing the work of God in his life, calling him into pastoral ministry. Anne supported Shelton's decision and agreed that he needed to begin his theological studies. They moved miles away from the comfort of her hometown with their two young daughters to Jackson, Mississippi. Without even uttering a sigh, she accepted the hardship of living a life with meager means while her husband worked, studied, and prepared for whatever God had in store for them. Suffice it to say that she was a woman who delighted in the gift of life and all it offered—whether good or bad—knowing there was purpose to be found in both.

Anne and Connie arrived back at my clinic the next morning. Strangely enough, Anne could sense that I was being somewhat more reserved and guarded than I had been the day before. I began to chat with her prior to the biopsy. She still held fast to her idea that everything would turn out fine. Her children were grown and settled, and all she wanted to do now was spend as much time as possible with her longtime soul mate, Shelton.

Anne shared with me how they had first met in kindergarten. She had fallen in love with him instantly, although it took longer for her to realize it. She told me how their lives had never been better, happier, or more fulfilling than in the past few months. They had been spending much of their time watching their young grandchildren grow up. Doing this brought visions to their minds of their own past youth in both body and spirit, and it also brought back memories of their children growing up.

During the bone marrow biopsy, Anne kept audibly praying and praising the Lord for all the blessings she had received in her life and kept asking the Lord Jesus for his will to be done, whatever it might be. She would often quote Philippians 4:13, "I can do all things through Christ who strengthens me." Her faith was heartening: she knew from the depths of her soul that no matter the results, God had her best interest at heart. She prepared to head home after the procedure as if it had been just another typical day, all the while expressing eagerness to restart her volunteer work at Piedmont Medical Center as soon as possible.

While Anne was readying herself to leave after the bone marrow biopsy was completed, Connie asked if she could personally take the bone marrow sample to the hospital.

"Of course," I replied. "That would give us the results sooner so that we can decide what the next step should be. That would be of great help; otherwise, I'd have to drive up to the hospital to drop it off myself."

The following day, Dr. Rob Thomas called me. The melancholy in his voice alerted me to the fact that something was wrong before he even finished his first sentence. "Kashyap," he began in a disturbed voice, "I know you have just seen Anne and her husband, Shelton. Besides being good friends of ours, Shelton also happens to be our pastor. Out of great concern, Connie had personally stopped by my office to drop off Anne's bone marrow. Unfortunately, I have found that her bone marrow is full of blast. She has developed acute myeloid leukemia."

Rob's voice sounded very low, and it was audibly trembling. I didn't have to discuss anything else. How could I? Anne was expecting to come to me to get a clean bill of health so that she could join her husband on his trip to Taiwan. Not to mention it was Valentine's Day, which also happened to be Shelton's birthday. I was in a moral dilemma as to how I could break the news to a family that had been living happily for so long. With a heavy heart, I placed the call asking them to come to my office.

Later that afternoon Anne arrived with both her daughter and her husband. Dr. Shelton Sanford was a senior pastor and one of the leading inspirational figures for thousands in the Southeast. The Sanford family had been connected with the healthcare field as well. Anne had been a volunteer at the Piedmont Medical Center for the past decade. With her perennial and inspirational smile, she was known to almost all of the hospital's employees. Connie was an ER nurse, and Shelton, through his role as pastor, had helped numerous families deal with bad news. Today was going to be a trying and testing time for them all. In the past, all three had helped people face bad news with optimism and faith. Today, they would be the ones who needed help.

Years of experience are utterly worthless when you have to break such bad news to someone. No matter how much you try, nothing can ever prepare you. Despite having done it thousands of times before, I've found it never gets any easier. Each time I always find it difficult to conceal my own emotions, and far too often, I have to turn my head to hide the solitary tear that trickles out of my eye.

I could see the anxious tears already flowing from Connie's eyes as soon as I entered the room. In spite of all of our collective wishful thinking that Anne merely had megaloblastic anemia–something that I could have easily handled with B12 injections–the stark and harsh reality of life stared back into my eyes. Anne had acute myeloid leukemia. It was an absolute certainty, and there was no way I could postpone the discussion with her and the family. I held Anne's hand as I slowly began to speak.

"Anne, your bone marrow reveals that you have acute myeloid leukemia."

The news dropped like a stone in a pond. The ripple effect of what that could possibly mean was reflected on their faces as their minds processed my words. I paused before I went on.

"While the news isn't good, I want to make you aware that this isn't a hopeless situation." Once again, I stopped for a brief moment as this sank in.

"There are treatment options available; adding the fact that you are relatively young and healthy to your determination to fight means that we have a very legitimate shot at beating this."

I had to pause again to regain my composure. As I saw everyone's cheeks begin to glisten with fresh tears, I felt helplessness overcome me as it never had before. In front of me was a family that always stood up to the occasion of helping anyone and everyone who needed help. Here before me was a renowned religious and spiritual leader, who by his mere touch and prayers had uplifted the spirits of many distressed and needy individuals. Here was Connie, who had witnessed countless life-threatening emergencies and deaths, carried out cardiopulmonary resuscitations, and consoled and assisted the sufferers from all walks of life through physical and emotional pain. And finally, here was Anne, whose simple smile had helped many forget their anxieties and anguish. They were set at a new juncture of life, about to enter a roller coaster of turmoil over the next few months. They didn't know what tomorrow would bring, where they would be, or what shape they would be in. Everyone in the room knew that life had come to a screeching halt and a new, unknown path with a foggy and unclear future was unfolding before them. For a moment, everybody in the room started mentally exploring their own worlds. Connie started recalling her own memories of leukemic patients with life-threatening infections reporting to the ER and then not making it through hospitalization. Shelton started remembering numerous occasions when he had led prayer vigils for his church members and followers for whom he soon after had to officiate funeral services.

And yet, Anne was surprisingly calm. She imagined that she was driving on a glorious autumn day through the beautiful Blue Ridge Mountains where her family had a lovely mountain home. She saw the scenic road encased in the vivid and beautiful colors of fall. She saw the changing landscapes created by falling leaves. And then, she suddenly came upon a thick patch of fog–fog so thick that she felt blindfolded. All of her dreams of one day traveling across the globe with Shelton, spreading messages of peace and prayers, lay shattered. All that remained was the promise of pain, suffering, and eventually saying goodbye to everything, even her children and grandchildren. Anne already knew too much about leukemia. Her brother had been an oncologist and an avid

researcher at Johns Hopkins University. He had an incredibly brilliant career with background training at Yale and Harvard. He also
was instrumental in initiating a transplant program at the University of Wisconsin. He had been involved in one of the first ever
bone marrow transplants in the country. And her dear brother, Dr.
William H. Burns, who had devoted his entire life to researching
leukemia and bone marrow transplantation, had died just three
years earlier from a massive stroke.

While I was grappling with my sudden mental block and was
searching for words of encouragement, optimism, and solace, Anne
broke the silence and began speaking.

"I am not afraid. The Lord allowed me to have leukemia for a
purpose. I have always trusted him, and I know I am in his loving
arms. I have a strong family. My husband and I have been together
for almost forty years. Now will come the time of patience and
testing. But I know we'll navigate the tough and challenging times
that are facing us. I have a bright future to look forward to," Anne
said, and then she began to pray aloud. "Oh, Lord, I thank you
today for giving me this opportunity to serve you through my own
suffering. I am thankful to you, Lord, once again for choosing me
over someone else who may not have as strong a faith and family
as I do. I am truly indebted to you, my Lord, and from now on, I
will be at your service always."

I was stunned at Anne's faith and composure. She had accepted
her disease without any further questioning. While I always thought
my wealth of experience that stemmed from working on three
different continents and interacting with people of all walks of life
and faith had developed within me a mature outlook, I felt timid
in front of her great and graceful attitude. We all slowly regained
our composure.

It was Connie's turn. She broke the silence. "Now what, Dr. Patel? Where do we go from here? When can we start her treatment? Can we do it in Rock Hill, or do you recommend that we take her to a tertiary care center?"

"Well, I think she is best served by going to a leukemia expert for treatment. While I personally have been involved in caring for many patients with leukemia, I honestly think she will receive the best care from someone who does it on a daily basis. We have several options. You can go to Charlotte, Greenville, Charleston, or maybe Duke Medical Center. Tell me what's most convenient, and I'll arrange for admittance there."

"Where would you go if it was your own family member who needed help?" Connie asked directly. "My mom's brother, Dr. Burns, was a famous transplant physician at Johns Hopkins University. He was a tremendous resource for all of us, but he passed away three years ago. Therefore, we count very heavily on your opinion. What do you recommend? I am confident you will guide us to the right place."

"Connie, your question isn't an easy one for me to answer, but I see where you're going. If it were my own family member, I would go to Gary Spitzer in Greenville, South Carolina. I know Gary personally. He is incredibly caring and practically a genius in the field of leukemia and lymphoma. He has treated several of my patients in the past, and they were all extremely satisfied. On top of it, like me, he's the sort of man who doesn't keep private time for himself. He will be accessible 24/7 via his cell phone."

"Would you please contact him as soon as possible? We're anxious to begin treatment. In addition, can you at least tell us what types of treatment and what side effects we'll likely face?" Connie asked.

I had worked in several different renowned hospitals and organizations dealing with leukemia and bone marrow transplants in both the US and England. Five years of my life had been spent dealing with blood diseases; with that experience, I started to explain statistics with a measure of optimism.

"Anne, I don't want to minimize the extent of treatments and side effects you'll be facing. Based on my experience, I think that you'll need to be in the hospital for at least three weeks each month for the next five to six months. Your immune system will be nearly destroyed in the hope that the new cells replacing old, abnormal, leukemic cells will be healthy and will build your immune system anew. The first treatment will be aimed at destroying all the leukemia cells that are in your system. If we succeed in achieving that mission, then the rest of the treatment cycles will be used to eliminate any possible microscopic cancerous cells remaining. The first treatment is termed the induction cycle, since we intend to induce remission. While this is a more generic description, I'll leave the detailed discussion to Gary Spitzer and his team since he will be more familiar with the specific side effects of the regimen he will choose to administer."

I politely withheld any more discussions due to the fact that Shelton and Anne had already started revealing anxiety on their faces. Plus, Gary was doing leukemia treatment day in and out, and it was only fair for Anne and Shelton to hear from the most qualified doctor what the likely complications and response rates would be.

Even so, Connie wasn't about to let me off that easy. "One last question," she said. "What is the likelihood of cure?"

"That is very hard to predict," I replied. "In all probability, Anne will acquire remission fast. The timeframe for cure remains with her body's response to treatment. She has almost a seventy percent chance of achieving remission. Once her body clears the leukemia after the induction cycle treatment, her immune system will struggle with leukemia cells for survival. Faith, prayers, confidence, family support, and blessings from the Almighty, in addition to the chemotherapy that we infuse, will eventually decide her fate," I continued. "I also would like to give you a word of caution about Gary. While I am an overt optimist, he is more of a realistic pragmatist. Don't be discouraged if you hear anything negative from him, as he is always guarded. Short of that, everything will be fine."

I took a short break from speaking to allow them to absorb all that had been said.

"Anne and Shelton, I would suggest that you go home and try to rest a bit. I know it's hard to absorb all the information we have discussed. You all are on the receiving end today. Let this information sink in and allow yourselves time to come up with questions that need to be answered. I believe you have plenty to think about."

I then placed a call to Gary Spitzer. "Gary, this is Kashyap. I need a special favor. I saw this delightful lady two days ago for thrombocytopenia. Wishfully, I was hoping she had megaloblastic anemia so that I could cure her anemia and thrombocytopenia. However, she turned out to have acute myeloid leukemia. Would you be willing to help?"

"You know me, Kashyap. I've tried my best to help your patients. But I also know that you infuse a lot of hope in them and that I end up giving them a reality check, sometimes at the expense of displeasing them and becoming the bad guy." A silent moment passed. "What is her name, and how soon does she want to come down here?" Gary said with his characteristic Australian accent. He turned from the receiver and started talking to his nurse. "Wendy! Kashyap is on the other line. He has this delightful lady that he wants to send our way. Do you think we can get her in today or tomorrow?"

Wendy must have told him that either day was doable. He spoke to me again. "Do you want to send her today or tomorrow? Also, you can pass along my cell number and tell her that I will be very happy to answer any questions she has."

"All right. I will let you know when she can come, Gary. Thanks for your help." And with that, I ended the conversation.

Anne, Shelton, and Connie left my office with heavy hearts. Even then, I was sure that the severity and gravity of the situation hadn't fully sunk in. It seemed as if heavy weights were chained to their feet as they slowly walked out of the office. I walked with them, gently holding Anne's hand, not knowing what shape and spirit she would be in when she returned. No one could have offered worse news on Valentine's Day. Life had rotated one hundred eighty degrees for them all.

Shelton's plan to go to Taiwan had been cancelled, and he decided to devote as much time as possible to Anne's care. Despite these sudden and overwhelming developments, Anne was the least worried of us all. Since she had already decided to leave every inch of her existence in God's hands, none of the discussions ever bothered her. She even said, "Lord, you are my Shepherd, and I will follow wherever you lead me. If you want me to come to you, I will happily relinquish everything on this earth to be with you in the heavenly abode that you have prepared for me. Above all, my trust is in you."

She went home to her modest house in Rock Hill and sat with Shelton on the lovely brick patio in her backyard. Shelton brought out their iron fireplace and got a flame going. Although the evening was somewhat cold, they both had enough going on in their minds to stop them from noticing either the cold in the air or the heat from the fire. Anne and Shelton had lived an idyllically happy existence up to that point. They had spent many years of their life in their wonderful home, sharing so many good times with their children and grandchildren.

But today, everything was different. As Anne looked up at a dark winter sky, she wondered how often she would have the chance to sit on her patio with her loved one near while she gazed up toward heaven. She absorbed Shelton's unspoken anxieties like a sponge. She could feel a weak yet cruelly chill breeze blowing through the leaves of the evergreen spruces in the backyard. She listened to the scratchy sounds the branches made as the wind moved through them. The familiar sound was oddly reassuring. She thought of *The Inferno, which she had read when young, and remembered Dante Alighieri's famed quotation in the introduction—one that, until today, she had never truly understood:*

> *"Midway upon the journey of our life*
> *I found myself within a forest dark,*
> *For the straightforward pathway had been lost."*

CHAPTER 2

# THE FLASHBACKS

*I have always believed that whatever good or bad fortune may come our way we*
*can always give it meaning and transform it into something of value.*
—HERMANN HESSE

ANNE LOOKED AT THE BARREN dogwood trees and the dry,
flowerless azaleas that formed a natural fence around her backyard. Dogwoods, azaleas, and gardenias… her mind slipped back
to almost forty years ago, to the distant past and her first romance.
She remembered how Shelton had proposed to her beneath a
dogwood tree surrounded by azaleas and fragrant gardenias. Her
life was captured in those moments—so much so that after moving
to Rock Hill, they decided to create a similar landscape to help
keep that precious moment alive in their minds forever.

Her mind skipped further back to the day almost forty-seven
years ago when she had first laid eyes upon Shelton. She had
instantly liked him and, in that phase of childhood innocence,
would play with him daily. Anne and Shelton were in the same
class in kindergarten. Both of their families knew each other very
well. Anne was born into the prominent Burns family of Macon,
Georgia, and raised "with a silver spoon in her mouth." Though her

family enjoyed the lifestyle of the rich and famous southern elite, they were quite modest. Shelton's family was equally well known for its prosperity and philanthropy. Even in those days, Anne's grandparents had the luxury of a chauffeur at a time when even owning a car was a farfetched dream for many. For the first three years of their childhood friendship, they enjoyed their innocent moments of love by playing with each other almost all the time. Vacation times were even shared by their families.

Anne distinctly remembered an episode when both families had gone to the Blue Ridge Mountains. Out of the blue, Anne's dog bit Shelton. Barely eight at the time, Shelton had felt embarrassed and somewhat humiliated. Anne couldn't believe she would feel her loyalties and affection divided between her friend and her dog.

When middle school rolled around, Shelton moved on in his life in his own way. Anne thought she had lost him forever. While neither of them understood what love was at the time, they both knew they sincerely missed each other. A few years passed, and the distance remained.

Upon meeting up again in high school, Anne couldn't believe how her childhood friend had finally come back into her life. This time they were both mature and were very conscious of non-verbal cues and communications with each other. They wanted to make up for lost time. They conveyed more through their eyes than through words spoken.

Anne's mind wandered back to one beautiful late winter morning with the sky a shade of crystal clear blue and the sun shining in all its warm golden glory. Winter was unusually warm that year, and for a week, temperatures soared in the seventies and eighties. All the plants and birds had misread the rising temperature as the arrival of spring, flowers had started blooming, and birds had started chirping musical tunes pleasing to the ears. Anne was waiting for her class to

begin. For some strange reason, she was by herself in a corner surrounded by beautiful azaleas in full bloom, giving a romantic pink
color to their surroundings. In front of her was a beautiful dogwood
tree with gorgeous white flowers but virtually no leaves. She saw
Shelton softly walking towards her with his hands behind his back
and his eyes cast down. Even though he was shy, a radiant smile lit
up his face. He inched very close to Anne to the point that she felt
a little embarrassed. Fortunately, they were by themselves in the
remote corner of the school grounds. Silently, Shelton brought his
hand forward, and in it was a beautiful red rose.

"Anne, I love you!" He said gently. "Here is a reflection of my
feelings. Please accept it as an offering of my heart."

Shelton was opening his own heart in front of this beautiful
young girl with long, flowing, brunette hair. He didn't have to con-
vince her of his true love. She knew all along how much Shelton
liked and admired her. Still, she was not ready to believe this could
come so fast and in such a pleasant way. Were her eyes and ears
playing tricks on her? It was as if she had waited her whole life for
that moment. An absence of more than a few years hadn't dimmed
the love she felt for him. From the first time she saw Shelton in
kindergarten, she had practically fallen in love with him. Those
innocent feelings of affection had blossomed into true love. It was
providence that it was Valentine's Day. The weather was perfect; the
azaleas and English dogwoods with their fragrant flowers made
their surroundings a picture of romance. The grass was green, and
a red cardinal was singing its pleasant song overhead.

Anne's cheeks turned pink as she blushed. Her face felt warm
in the cold, gentle, early spring breeze that wafted through the
thick pines behind her on the high school grounds. She could
hear symphonies of birds celebrating their first romantic moments.
Gardenias on the ground were in full bloom, adding very sweet

fragrant aromas. It was as if nature and the Almighty were showering blessings on these innocent teenage lovers. Anne gently but shyly reciprocated.

"I love you too, Shelton." She held his hands in hers and kissed his cheek. She took the rose in her hands, smelled it, and then ran away. Surprisingly, Shelton wasn't the only shy one.

Her life was perfect. She had found her soul mate. As time went by, Anne was becoming a beautiful young woman with thick brunette hair and a perfect round face.

Both the Burns and Sanford families had sensed the strong feelings translating into love between Shelton and Anne. The elite community in Macon was also a very close-knit group. Anne's parents had guessed with whom her heart lay. One fine morning, Anne's dad asked her to sit down for a talk. Anne's mom was also there, listening to the exchange between father and daughter.

"Anne, may I ask you a very private question?"

"Of course, Dad! You can ask me anything you want," Anne replied.

"Do you like Shelton?" As per his nature, his question was very straightforward and direct.

"You mean Sanford?" she replied. Anne was shy and certainly not prepared for this sudden surprise.

"Yes, I am talking about Shelton Sanford. Do you love him?" he continued.

"Dad, why are you asking me this question all of a sudden? And why today?"

Anne was unsure whether she should reveal her feelings.

"Anne, dear! Your father is asking this because we are seriously considering approving your relationship with Shelton. Before we agree to endorse your relationship, we want to ask you and Shelton for a favor," her mom interjected, knowing how uncomfortable Anne was in continuing the conversation.

"What is it? What can we do to make you both happy?"

"Well, you know, nowadays students are not completing their high school studies and are dropping out right and left. We just want to make sure that Shelton attends at least one year of college before we give our blessings on your marriage!"

"Don't worry, Mom. I'll talk to Shelton. It's a done deal. I know him well. He will do anything for us to be together." Anne's face was fully flushed. That was all it took for her to start dreaming about their wedding.

The scenes of Anne's life were slipping back and forth in her mind again. Her years had been filled to the brim with fun and joy. All of a sudden, she had awakened to a harsh new reality. She wasn't just worried about herself. She was greatly concerned about Shelton. They had been together for almost fifty years—both literally and figuratively—and now out of the blue, she felt as if a tornado was ripping apart all of the precious relationships and things she held dear.

She had been more attached to Shelton than his shadow. After their wedding, Shelton had taken over his family's business of furniture trading. However, she always felt that Shelton's heart was in teaching God's Word. Within a couple of years of running the business, the entire nation experienced a serious economic downturn. Shelton had to sell everything—literally every small asset from his business. That, however, turned out to be a blessing in disguise.

Shelton was very sensitive to Anne's needs. Having both been born into wealthy families, neither had ever experienced any real hardships in life. The loss of the business was the first setback that either of them had ever suffered, and it came at the tender age of twenty-five.

Shelton reluctantly and hesitantly approached his wife. "Anne, you know me. My heart isn't in running a business and earning money. I believe that the Lord is leading us to a different destination. I want to quit doing business and go to a seminary. I want to become a pastor. Could you be a pastor's wife?"

There was a brief silence between the two.

Shelton quickly filled the silence. "Don't worry; if you don't want me to do this, I'm sure that I can find some other business that will interest me more!"

Above all else, Shelton didn't want to upset Anne.

"I wasn't hesitating, dear. I was just wondering which seminary would be best. When do you want to start?"

The Sanford family moved to Jackson, Mississippi, barely making do with $100 a month and some savings that they had accumulated over the years. After completion of training, they lived for a time in a small town in Mississippi and then finally relocated to Rock Hill in 1985. The rest was history.

Scenes of her life continued to flash through her mind: memories of their wedding, their first child, and the births of each of their grandchildren. The memories were passing at speeds that seemed like millions of miles per second. It appeared as if her entire life was streaming by her in the blink of an eye. In thirty short minutes, Anne mentally viewed picture postcards of the moments that made up forty years of her life. The landscapes had changed entirely. What used to be a field of green was now replaced by the barren winter that was looming in front of her.

What mattered most to Anne now was remaining a strong witness of her faith and continuing to meet the needs of her family as she had previously managed to do. All vacation planning, upcoming events, minute details, and worries of everyday life had abruptly lost their footholds in her mind, and at the moment seemed alien to her. Only her health remained relevant. Exactly forty years ago was the St. Valentine's Day when Shelton had bought her the beautiful red rose. The same dogwood tree, the same bunch of azaleas and fragrant gardenias that were always bringing pleasant memories in the spring along with thoughts of the tender moments of Shelton's proposing to her, were now warring with the cold landscape and the winter blues.

Anne continued to sit and think—shaking the dust off old memories that had been tucked into the recesses of her heart. Fifty plus years after having met Shelton, she was going to start on another new journey. Only this time, she wasn't sure how long their companionship would last. She was sure that God would be with her the whole way. She began thinking this day was the time to intentionally order all her steps. So many people had enriched her life, and it was important they knew how very thankful she was for them. This was the season to love, give, share, and return all things borrowed. No regrets—no debts.

Beside her, Shelton was still blankly looking up at a dark sky illuminated with dim stars. He was searching for a ray of hope, but all he could see was the dark blanket above him. Their silent communication was interrupted every now and then by a gentle breeze, and every so often the lights of an airplane on its way to Charlotte would flash in the darkness.

Shelton had counseled and consoled hundreds of congregational members throughout his career as a senior pastor. Cancer was nothing new to him. He had visited and prayed at the bedsides of some of his closest personal friends. He had invoked the Holy Spirit through his prayers countless times. With his commanding yet soothing voice, his sermons had uplifted the emotions of thousands of church followers. Today though, he was lost in the vast wilderness that constituted life. He was looking for direction from above, or indeed, any ray of optimism. He was praying for the blessings of the Almighty. In the serene, supernal, evening winter sky, both his and Anne's spirits were flying, looking for solace in the darkness. Their daughter, Connie, whose face could not conceal the extent of emotional turmoil that had grasped her, finally interrupted their silent communication. Without her make-up, her face was bright red and still shining from the remains of dried tears. Connie had cooked a delicious meal, and she came to get both of her parents for dinner.

"Is it all over?" Shelton was asking himself and God at the same time. He briefly looked at Anne's beautiful face. She still had the same youthful charms that had attracted him so many decades ago, and her beauty seemed ageless. Or maybe he never looked at only her sole physical beauty; he simply saw her as a true soul mate who ideally would be with him for life without age or disease ever interrupting.

"Mom, dinner is ready. Please come in," Connie said, "and Dad, you too. The temperature is dropping, and I don't want Mom to catch a cold. For all we know, it could culminate in pneumonia."

Shelton thought to himself, "Is this how my life is going to be from now on?"

Anne didn't seem concerned at all. She came in and joined the family at the table. Following their usual routine, they all thanked the Lord for being there with them and prayed before they started their dinner. Sadly, a newfound tension hung over all conversations at the table that night.

# CHAPTER 3

# THE BATTLE
# BEGINS

*When praying for healing,*
*ask great things of God and expect great things from God.*
*But let us seek for that healing that really matters,*
*the healing of the heart, enabling us to trust God simply,*
*face God honestly, and live triumphantly.*
—ARLO F. NEWELL

THE NEXT DAY, ANNE, CONNIE, and Shelton drove to St. Francis Hospital in Greenville, SC, to start what would be the next chapter in their lives. Everything for them had changed in the flicker of a moment. Just the other day, Anne and Shelton were planning to go to Taiwan together. They were dreaming of having a wonderful time in Asia, the cradle of Buddhism, among a melting pot of different religions of the world. Instead, they were heading on a journey that had been started by many yet finished by few.

Anne was admitted to a special room at St. Francis. Dr. Spitzer came in and introduced himself.

"Hello, young lady! I am Gary Spitzer. It seems Kashyap was absolutely right when he told me that you are a delightful lady. I will be treating you for leukemia. Dr. Patel has already explained to me in elaborate detail what you have and what needs to be done. As a first order of business, we need to carry out lots of tests to determine how healthy your heart, liver, and lungs are so that we can decide which type of chemotherapy should be used. I will also ask our team to insert a tube near your collarbone so that we can infuse chemotherapy without hurting you too much. I'm sure you have lots of questions."

"Yes, we do indeed," Connie interjected. "What type of chemotherapy do you plan to use and within what frame? Also, how many cycles of treatment will you be doing, and what kind of side effects do you usually see?"

"Let me explain in detail where we go from here," Dr. Spitzer said. "For the first treatment round, we will be using two different chemicals: daunorubicin, which is red in color and cytarabine, which is clear. We will be infusing these chemicals over the next seven days through the tube that we are going to insert. We will then allow two weeks for your blood counts to recover. Wendy, my nurse, will be doing a bone marrow test to see if you are in remission. Before doing any additional treatments, you may be able to go home for a week or so and let Dr. Patel carry out normal follow-up tests."

Dr. Spitzer had more to say. "Bear in mind that chemotherapy is a fancy word for poison. My goal is to aim these poisons towards the target of harmful cells. As hard as I'll try to preserve healthy cells, quite a few will also be killed during treatment, which in turn will cause side effects. As far as side effects are concerned, you will probably feel nauseous. We will try to minimize that by giving you around-the-clock anti-nausea medications. When your blood counts drop, you may catch infections, start bleeding, or feel tired—depending upon which blood cells are affected. We do have remedies for correcting such. Unfortunately, you will lose your beautiful hair, but it will grow back when we are done. You may develop rashes here and there. Your stomach may get upset. Your heart function will weaken with the red drug."

"How do people deal with all these side effects, Dr. Spitzer? Are these too much to go through?" Connie asked, looking quite concerned.

Before Dr. Spitzer could answer, Anne did. "The Lord Jesus will help us sail through them," she said. "I know he chose me for leukemia so that I can bear witness and testimony for his glory and inspire others who go through this journey." She was the least concerned about the side effects of anyone present, including Dr. Spitzer. She knew in her heart that the Lord would be with her the whole time and that this was just a small bump on the road of her journey of life.

"Well, on that note, let me start ordering some tests for you, and hopefully we can begin your treatment tomorrow. I will be checking up on you at least once or twice a day or as often as needed."

Gary then turned towards his nurse and said, "Wendy, would you please order an echocardiogram, pulmonary function tests, routine blood chemistries, and the other necessary tests so that we can start Anne's treatment tomorrow?"

"Okay, I'll take care of it. I'll also coordinate the PICC line placement for her chemotherapy," Wendy replied.

"One final note before I leave," Gary said and paused briefly. "Do you have any siblings who are in good health?"

"Yes, I have a sister and two brothers who are alive. You already know one of my brothers died three years back from a massive stroke. Like you, he was also a renowned leukemia expert," Anne replied. "Does it matter?" She couldn't understand why Gary wanted to know about her siblings.

"Can we get them to see their doctors and check their blood types in detail so that we can consider a bone marrow transplant if they match your type?" Gary asked.

Anne was shocked! "Is my leukemia that serious?" For the first time, she began feeling intense anxiety.

"I didn't mean that," Gary replied. "I just want to keep all options open. In case your leukemia doesn't respond the way we desire, we'll need for you to undergo a bone marrow transplant."

Her first day in the hospital was very hectic. Approximately every thirty minutes, someone new came into her room and either checked her temperature and pulse, did a blood test, or wheeled her down to the X-ray department or radiology for more tests. Wendy stopped by a couple of times as well. Anne was exhausted by the end of the day. Shelton and Connie were by her side the entire time.

To her amazement, Anne felt that she wanted some time to herself that night. She knew her journey through cancer was going to be trying, and the only way through this minefield was to set her mind on the Lord Jesus every step and every moment. She had been so overwhelmed the past few days that she really had not taken time for a deep, intimate, one-on-one conversation with God. She decided to utilize her time in the hospital to commune with God.

On the first day after her diagnosis, prior to commencement of her treatment, Anne began writing a journal to God.

### Tuesday, February 15, 2005

*Dear God,*

*Today you and I are getting ready to start on an exciting adventure, and I am so thankful to have you with me and to know you are in control. Thank you for choosing me to have leukemia. My utmost desire is to glorify you in every way and through each event. Already you have blessed me in so many ways. I am claiming Isaiah 43 as my dearest. I love all of your Word, but for now these are my favorites. Yesterday you gave me Matthew 11:28–30, and as I read, Jesus said, "Are you tired? Come to me, get away with me, and you will receive your life." I have been so tired. Truly I am thankful for this time alone with you to be refreshed and to receive strength from you. Thank you for all your blessings throughout the years. I am most excited about walking along with you the next few months. I do not want to miss anything you want me to learn through this. I know the treatment will be hard, but I want to be strong and to be a good witness for you. Show me what you desire me to learn. Thank you for loving me! All I can say over and over again is that you love me and you are with me. We have prayed for your direction to the right place for treatment, and we really feel you are leading us to Greenville. Please let this be the best place for me. Let me do great with the treatment and protect me from infection. I pray these seven days of treatment will put this cancer into remission and that it will be clear sailing from then on. I pray I will have "minimal to none" side effects. I love you, Lord, and I am thankful you are with me. I will sign off for now, but we will talk later. I especially want to be a witness to my family, friends, and strangers.*

*I love you and thank you, Lord.*

*Anne*

True to his word, Dr. Spitzer stopped by to check on her, and Wendy also came by later to briefly explain the next steps.

"Anne, we have just about completed all the needed testing. We still have to evaluate your heart and lung function. Once we ascertain that your cardiac and pulmonary functions are acceptable, we will start your chemotherapy. You will be getting two separate infusions of chemotherapy drugs. These drugs are actually cell poisons, and they interfere with the cell division and replication cycle of leukemia cells. As much damage as they will cause to leukemia cells, some normal cells will also be killed despite being innocent bystanders–something similar to collateral damage. You may experience some side effects in your mouth, gut, and blood cells."

"I'm sure that I am going to be fine. As long as the Lord Jesus is with me, I will sail through this. I had a long conversation with him last night, and he assured me of his presence through this illness," Anne replied, confident in the power of her faith and trust in Jesus.

Wendy continued, "Anne, if you develop any fevers, rashes, chills, or any unusual feelings anywhere in your body, please ring the bell hanging by the side of your bed and call for help. I would rather you call more often than not, as sometimes you may be developing a side effect that may be very serious, and prompt action may help."

'I certainly will ring if I need any help," she replied.

Later that evening, Anne developed a fever. As instructed, she called for help. One of the nurses stopped by and tested her blood for infection. An antibiotic infusion was ordered to prevent any possible dissemination of infection. Leukemia had weakened Anne's immune system so badly that even a typical germ that would not otherwise harm a normal individual was causing fevers and infection in Anne's body.

Later that night, Anne had a strange feeling. This perhaps was the last night she was going to harbor the same blood cells in her body that had been part of her all these years. Of course, they had become mutated. Like terrorists who begin their lives as normal human beings but mutate and make it difficult for ordinary, God-loving humans to lead a normal life, these cancer cells had made it difficult for Anne's own blood cells to live naturally. She knew when the doctors infused the red and the clear poisons into her body the next day, those mutated cells would be destroyed forever. For one more night though, they were a part of her body. She prayed and then started journaling her own conversation with Jesus.

### Wednesday February 16, 2005

*Well, this has been an exciting day!! It has been a long one. I am tired and ready to call it a day. I have a fever now, and I pray it will go away. I know you can take it away, so please do so. I pray you will let them get the chemotherapy started early in the morning, the chest x-ray and echocardiogram done, and the line put in before noon. Let it all go well, and keep infection at bay. I know you have plans for me, to give me a hope and a future. You are with me as I fight this battle. I believe we can beat this. I so want to be a good witness for you. Please, please heal me, Lord.*

*Thank you, my Father and Comforter.*

*Good night. I love you.*

*Anne*

Anne's journey into the land of the unknown began the next morning. Her doctors placed a tube in one of the major blood vessels below her left collarbone through an incision under the skin. This tube was supposed to be kept in until she had completed all of her treatment. Anne took this new addition to her body as an ornament, rather like an oddly worn necklace. She thought that the small tube would serve to keep reminding her of the Lord Jesus all the time.

Once again, the same chores that she went through the day before were repeated again. Anne was wheeled down to the cardiopulmonary lab for an ultrasound test of her heart and lung functioning. With her pleasant smiles, Anne was winning everyone's heart and leaving behind fond memories wherever she went. The good news was that her heart and lungs were very strong for her age and, without much difficulty or side effects, she should be able to withstand any type of strong chemicals capable of damaging her heart.

Nancy, one of the nurses involved in her care, came to her room and explained her chemo treatment again. "Mrs. Sanford, today we will start your treatment. I have a small bag of saline infused with a chemical that will prevent you from getting sick. I am going to hang it first for about fifteen minutes. Once this infusion is complete, I will hang two different cell killer poisons, or chemotherapy, on this IV pole and slowly infuse them through the tube next to your collarbone. I believe Dr. Spitzer and Wendy have already explained the possible side effects. Let me know if you experience any, and we'll see what we can do to alleviate them."

The liquids and the chemicals began to slowly drip into Anne's blood. She started praying as the poisons were infused into her body. She set out visualizing what was going on inside her body. She imagined the chemicals multiplying into multitudes of small droplets and attaching themselves to large, overgrown, hideous-looking leukemia cells. She also started visualizing that the same chemicals were converting themselves into ambrosia and were shielding the normal cells of her mouth, gut, and blood to prevent any ill effects on her body. To her surprise, she didn't feel any different than normal, despite having poisons placed in her blood. She continued praying and held firm to her faith that the Lord was truly her Shepherd and was helping her sail through the wild terrains of leukemia treatment.

The first day of actual treatment was full of action, with Anne trying to adjust to her new way of life. So far, she had given her life to the priority of serving ailing humanity. Now it was her turn to start receiving from her family and others. Unlike most ordinary human beings, Anne didn't see any adversities in her life. She took her ailment as a blessing that would allow her to be in constant shelter and touch with her God. So great was her acceptance of her disease that she continually thanked God for having chosen her for leukemia. Throughout the infusion of poisonous chemicals, Anne kept praying for the Lord's will to be done. Despite being tired and fatigued after a hectic day, with nurses visiting her every few minutes to ensure that everything was in the right order, Anne chose to continue her dialogue with the Lord Jesus. She was still running a low-grade fever.

### Thursday, February 17, 2005

*Dear Lord,*

*This is a wonderful day, for it is the day you have made and the first day of my chemo. I am so thankful to begin the process of killing this disease. They are coming in later with the final report for last week's bone marrow test, and I'm expecting good news! I pray I will have no infection during this entire time and that this cancer will be in remission after the induction phase of the treatment. Thank you, Lord, that I can trust you, for you alone know what is best for me. Thank you that you have forgiven me of all my sins. I rejoice in knowing that you love me and are in complete control of my circumstances. I am thankful for all of my wonderful family—especially Connie, Lucy, Palmer, and Shelton. Thank you for the strength you have given me. I love you beyond words.*

*In Jesus' name,*

*Anne*

Anne's first day of treatment had been rather uneventful with the exception of the low-grade fever. Dr. Spitzer and Wendy came for rounds rather early on day two.

"Anne, I have some good news. Your bone marrow does not reveal any evidence of adverse prognostic risk factor. What this means is that you are likely to respond to the treatment and stay in remission. Also, your blood tests didn't reveal any infections. Perhaps your fever was due to the leukemia itself, and as we kill more leukemia cells, your fever should improve. There is only a bit of bad news. It appears that you had some features of pre-leukemia before all this began. This feature worries me some. Short of this, everything seems to be in our favor."

"But Dr. Spitzer, I didn't have any symptoms of pre-leukemia. Does it arise just like that?" Anne asked curiously.

"Unfortunately, I'm afraid so! Acute leukemia does appear without any warning signs," he replied.

"Maybe that's what Jesus had planned for me. Is there a reason why I feel so weak and tired?" Anne then asked. Although there were no specific troubles thus far, she lacked energy to concentrate and focus.

"I was wondering about that. You are such an optimist and have such a strong personality that in spite of your red blood cell count and hemoglobin being so low, you don't appear to have any dreadful symptoms. You are feeling tired and weak because of anemia. Again, the leukemia cells are trying to push your normal blood cells out of your bone marrow and take over your body. It will be a while before normal cells can start reestablishing their control. Let me give you some blood so that you can start feeling better and enjoy your stay in this wonderful facility," Gary explained. Ultimately, it was the leukemia that was responsible for every adverse reaction in her body.

Anne didn't question anything in her life. She just accepted whatever she received with a grateful heart. Anne was excited that her fever was down and also that her symptoms were from leukemia and not from infections. She was also happy that although leukemia cells were trying to disrupt her life, some good souls had donated blood that would be used to help her feel better. Anne started seeing the battle going on in her body as one between chemotherapy and leukemia cells. She remained willing to accept whatever outcome God chose for her life.

### Friday, February 18, 2005

*Good morning, Lord,*

*Today is an exciting day for you and me. As you already know, I started my chemo at 11:00 this morning. Thank you that my fever went down and they were able to start the meds early. I also got two bottles of blood and feel much stronger. Lucy came today after school--what precious moments with Shelton and the children that you have blessed us with. They stood around my bed, read Isaiah 43:1–10, and prayed. These are special times I would never have experienced without this happening. I pray for your strength for Shelton and our children as we go through this. I want more than anything else for all of us to be drawn closer to you. As I look out at the mountains, I remember your mercies are new every morning and your faithfulness is great. When Lucy came, she brought lots of cards, food, and gifts from home. I am overwhelmed at everyone's kindness, love, and prayers. God, you are truly alive! You hear and answer prayers. I pray Connie will have a safe trip home and will enjoy these next two days with Will and J.R.*

### Saturday, February. 19, 2005

*Ruth and Wallace Tinsley came by last night, and Shelton had a good visit with them in the hallway. How sweet of them to come by. I really do appreciate it. It's Feb 19th now and a new day. As always, my prayer is that I will glorify you today through whatever comes my way. That is my utmost prayer through each step of the way. I pray my aging grandmother, Lucille, will let other people do for her and that she will be well taken care of. I love you, Lord, and thank you for allowing me to go through this. My soul's desire is to glorify you in and through these circumstances. Talk to you later....*

*It is Saturday night about 9:00, and I have had a great day. Lucy is with me tonight, and we are having fun. I just listened to my CD from the church, and Lucy read my cards from yesterday. Mail didn't get delivered today, so she read from mail I had previously received. It has hit me today that this is going to be a long-haul recovery, but I am determined to do all I can to win this battle. Bible verses have meant so much to me, and Shelton reads Isaiah 43:1–10 each day. Before he, Palmer, and Holly left tonight to go eat and head back to the hotel, he read Psalm 23. I know you are my Shepherd, and I want to be a good witness who brings glory and honor to you in all things. I pray especially that I will have no infection and, with the next infusion of chemo, I will be in remission. Help me to feel well the rest of the time and help me keep my eyes and trust on you. I have enjoyed my CD from the church today. Thank you for all you do to bring healing to me now. Be with Shelton--I know how much he hates to sit around. He is being so strong and so good to me.*

*I love you!!!*

*Anne*

**Sunday, February 20, 2005**

*Dear God,*

*I have had a wonderful day today. I sense how much people are interceding on my behalf. Lucy stayed with me last night, and we slept well. Shelton came early and brought me a biscuit and milkshake from Steak and Shake. He has been so loving and kind to me. He is truly wonderful, and we are so blessed to have had close to forty years together. He is very concerned about me. I can feel his great love for me. I also know of his great love for you! I want to be strong for him and the children. Palmer and Holly came over while Shelton was at church. Lucy was with me. Shelton brought us veggies from S and S Cafeteria, and Holly left to go home. Shelton bought some more pajamas for me, and Palmer washed them. I watched the Daytona 500. Palmer has been so sweet to be with me. I never thought my twenty-seven-year-old son would be taking me to the bathroom. He's a dear and so attentive. I just hate to ruin this time for Palmer and Holly. This is supposed to be a special time. I talked to Cille and Aunt Leila last night—they sounded good. Many friends are reaching out to Cille, which pleases me. Alice Pendergrass came by, and we had a nice visit. I feel really sad for her since she and her husband Jim have been here [in the hospital] for so long. He is so discouraged. This has been a good day, and I thank you for it. I know we will have some rough ones ahead of us, but I can get through anything as long as you are with me. Thank you for allowing me to serve you and help me to glorify you in all things. I love you, Lord. Goodnight for tonight. See you in the morning.*

*Love,*

*Your child, Anne*

## Monday, February 21, 2005

*Good morning, Lord,*

*This is my fourth morning of treatment. I had a good night. Palmer and I slept well. I have felt pretty good this morning. Shelton is here with me; bless his heart, I know how hard it is for him to sit still. My fourth treatment should start soon. I am claiming Isaiah 43:1–10. I am reading in Anne Graham Lotz's book this morning about you being my Abba Father. I claim this as your promise to me. Also, I remember all things work together for good to those who love the Lord and are called according to his purpose. Susan called this morning to say Courtney and Matt's little girl has Down's syndrome. Megan and Andy had a little boy, Michael Joseph, on Sunday the 20th. I feel well today and am so thankful that I don't have a fever. Please, please Lord, let me stay fever free and let this round put me into remission. I want to please and honor you in whatever happens. This is all for now. Talk to you later, and I'm praying constantly to you for strength.*

*Love you so much,*

*Your child Anne*

## Monday evening, February 21, 2005

*Dear God,*

*Here I am again, praising and thanking you for all you have done for me and for letting me get well. I have had a wonderful day. Connie got here early afternoon and gave me the best bed bath and washed my hair. I got new Laura Ashley pajamas from Aunt Leila, Nancy, and Suzie Williams. They are so nice. I ate some veggies for supper, and since then I have been feeling very well. Before supper Connie opened my mail for me. I got so much mail. I became tired after we had opened only about one-third of it. I will read the others tomorrow. You are so good to me, and I love you so. People's prayers, love, and gifts have meant so much. I can't believe the prayers. My white count is going down, which is a good thing. I plead with you and pray to you that this day chemo will put this cancer into remission and I won't have to have a bone marrow transfer. I know beyond a shadow of a doubt that this is where I should be. Yesterday the HR person from here (St. Francis hospital) was visiting in Rock Hill and went to Westminster Presbyterian Church. He came by this afternoon to introduce himself to us and to offer his services in any way. God, you think of everything. I am so happy to have my precious Connie here. She has organized everything and even put pictures on the wall. We will probably be known as the newly redone room. I love you, Lord, and so want to rest in you through all of this. I pray for the cancer to go into remission and that I will have no infections or fever of any kind.*

*Thank you, Father, for a great day. Talk to you in the morning.*
*Love, your child,*
*Anne*

## Tuesday, February 22, 2005

*Dear God,*

*Thank you so much for letting me feel so well on this fifth day of chemo. I love you and thank you for answering all prayers to feel well without fever. You are my Father; you give me so much strength. My precious Connie has just given me a wonderful bed bath and washed my hair. She is going home in a little while to be with Will and plans to be back on Friday. Shelton is on his way back over. I am overwhelmed at everyone's love and care. Connie finished reading me the cards today that had come in. All are so special—I truly love the Scripture ones. Precious Amy Lovelace called this morning and insisted on bringing all of us lunch. Connie met her at noon in the lobby and picked up a delicious feast. I give honor and glory to you for your great love and care as evidenced in many large and small ways. I pray for Courtney Sadler today—be with her through surgery and recovery, directing the doctors for her good. May Jim Pendergrass improve and have a better day. I want to thank you for allowing me to be drawn closer to you through this disease—focusing more and more on you. Your love, support, presence, strength and kindness and gentleness mean a lot to me.*

*I love you,*
*Anne*

*Dear Father,*

*Now it is Tuesday afternoon, and I have had a great day. This is my fifth day of chemo and thanks to you, I am feeling so well. I do pray that I will be in remission after the seven treatments and that I will be able to proclaim your glory and work in my life for many more years to come. I so want to be faithful and strong through all of this, especially for Shelton and the children. Palmer was so upset today, but he seems to have calmed down this evening. Please use this in the children's lives to draw them closer to you. Oh Lord, it is the desire of my heart that you would strengthen Shelton, Connie, JR, Will, Lucy, Kenny Burns, and Palmer and Holly. Keep their eyes on you so they will be reminded you are our ever-present help in our time of need. You have promised me in your Word that you love me, you are with me, and you will take me through every step of the way. I want to learn all you have for me to learn from this. You are my life! You have always done so much for me, and I have had the most wonderful life. My main prayer requests are that people will continue to intercede in prayer, praise, and thanksgiving on my behalf and that my cancer will go into remission after the seven treatments so I won't need a bone marrow transplant. If I do need a transplant, please let one of my brothers or sisters be a match. I thank you so much that my fever is good; I pray it will stay down and that I won't have any more sores or infection of any kind. Thank you, Lord, for everything. I do pray for a good night tonight. I also pray for the approach of little Molly's birth—may all go well for them. I pray the tests will be back soon. Thank you for Michael's birth too and that Vicki was able to be there with her. Remember how much I love you and want to be a testimony to your healing hand and power in my life. I'm signing off for the evening and will write more in the morning.*

*I love you,*

*Anne*

## Wednesday, February 23, 2005

*Good morning, Lord,*

*Thank you so much for taking me safely through another night and letting me feel so great. I know it is because of you and your strong love and care for me. I do love you so much and want to glorify you in all aspects of my life. You are amazing! I continue to put my trust in you through all of this. I know you are with me for I sense your presence throughout my waking hours. I feel like the crippled lamb in the story English sent me today. I thank you for all of the prayers that are spoken for me, all the encouraging cards, and for the love of friends and people I don't even know. It took Shelton over an hour this morning to open and read all of the cards that came yesterday. I feel so special. I know this sounds crazy, but if you hadn't allowed me to have cancer, I would never have experienced this love and peace from you. Palmer called, and his cabinets came early this morning, so they are unloading at his house. Michael will come next weekend and help him put them up. I do pray you will use this in Palmer's life and the other children's lives as well. I want to be healed so I can share your Word for many more years. I had not been diligent in my walk with you, Lord, but now you have my attention in a special way. I love you so much and long to obey and follow after you. Thank you so much for another good night and day. I'll sign off for now but will check in later.*

*I just thought of Becky Pritchard—may she fly safely today to Boston for Matt's wedding. Oh, Mandy has come to mind, Lord. Please help her so that she will not have a miscarriage. In all things, Father, may your will be done.*

*I love you,*
*Anne*

*Hello, Lord,*

*It's Wednesday night, and I want to thank you again for another wonderful day. Thank you that I have felt so good again. I do have a low-grade fever tonight, and I ask that it not rise any higher and that I will not have any infection. I pray that this first treatment series will put cancer in remission so I won't have to have a bone marrow transplant. I am thankful Molly got to go home today, and I pray for the whole family—may they feel your love upholding them. Thank you for godly parents for little Molly. I'm grieving so much for Merle and family in the loss of Greg. I pray you would comfort and strengthen them in a special way. I pray that Greg did know and love you and is with you in eternity now. May the family sense your sweet presence as you minister to their hurting hearts. I thank you that Mandy's baby is doing so well and that all is right with it. Give her an easy pregnancy and healthy baby. Thank you for transporting me through this adventure with you, Lord. I do fervently pray that this treatment will put me into remission and I will not have to have a bone marrow transplant. Help me to evade infection, fever, nausea, and anything else that would create complications in this fight toward healing and health. I talked to Sidney Robinson tonight; she has survived breast cancer and is doing so well now. She is a real encouragement to me. Thanks again so much for another wonderful day, and I pray I will rest well tonight and feel well in the morning. I know I am doing so well because you love and care for me! I do appreciate everyone's love and prayers.*

*Signing off for tonight.*

*One more thing, Sarah, one of the cleaning staff here, told me today she had placed me on the prayer list of her church and that they prayed for me. Such comments encourage me greatly. I love you.... good night.*

*Love,*

*Anne*

## Thursday, February 24th 2005

*Hello, Lord,*

*Here I am again tonight, praising you for another wonderful day. As I began my seventh day of treatment today, I thought I might feel badly—once again you have heard and answered my prayers. I feel great. I had the best night of rest. They gave me platelets today. Thank you, Lord, that my fever has been normal. I pray it will continue to be so. I pray I will have no infection anywhere and I will be in remission after this treatment of chemo. Shelton got me a grilled cheese at the deli for lunch. He bought me a milkshake this morning from Steak and Shake and a biscuit from Burger King. Palmer got in around two after I had my bed bath. The mail came shortly after that, and it was fun for Palmer to read and show me all of the cards and mail. It means so much to me for my family to read aloud the Scriptures that people have sent. Thank you, Lord, for all of your many blessings—though some may seem small, they are all powerful to me. Tonight Shelton picked up a turkey sandwich from McAlisters that I enjoyed immensely. Palmer and Shelton left at around 7:00 to go eat supper and go to the hotel. It is so nice that the church has given us the use of the hotel room so whoever comes can use it as the need arises. I thank you and praise you, Father, for all of your goodness to me. Please help me to be a strong witness for you, Father, in whatever the outcome will be. I trust you, Father, and thank you for all of your promises to me found in your Word. Help me to be able to recall them in my time of need. I pray for a good night of rest and to feel well. May all of my family rest well too; I know being at the hospital and away from home is hard on them. I also pray for the Crafts; I know their hearts are so heavy over Greg's death. I pray the service on Saturday will be uplifting and glorifying to you and comforting to the Crafts. I pray for Mrs. Baldwin in the death of her mother. Comfort her and her family too. I pray for little Molly as they all get settled into a routine at home, that she will make great strides. I pray also for Ethel's friend—may she improve to the point her doctors can remove life support. Father, I am so thankful that even in these hard times, I can trust you. I know you are a loving, caring, and peaceful God. Thank you again for another great day and help me to have a good night of rest. May I be free from fever and may the cancer reach remission stage soon. Thank you for your Word. I love you—good night.*

*Anne*

### Friday, February 25, 2005

*Thank you, Lord, so much for another great day. Today is a grand celebration because I had my last chemo treatment in this series. God, you are so good, and even today you made yourself known through the simple provision of a cake. During the night I thought it would be fun to celebrate the end of chemo today with a cake. I asked Nancy, my favorite nurse, if there was a bakery nearby, and she said, "Yes, is someone having a birthday?" I told her what I wanted it for, and she said she would get one for me when she got off work. I told her I could ask Shelton to get one when he called around 7:30 to see if I needed anything other than the milkshake and biscuit I had asked him to bring. I thought Palmer could stop by Bi-Lo and pick one up. When I mentioned this to Shelton, he responded by telling me that Frances Barnes and Mary John Sharpe had already left a beautiful pound cake for us in the hotel room. I couldn't believe it. My favorite kind, no less!!!*

*God, you are so good and so loving to me. I thank you for seeing me through all the days of chemo so well. I thank you from the bottom of my heart for each good hour you give me. I do thank you for all the blessings you have given me through this chemo treatment. I pray this round will put me into remission and that I won't have any infection or fever. I so want to glorify you, Lord, in everything concerning this cancer fight. I thank you for safe travel for everyone back and forth during this time. Bless Palmer now as he travels back to Atlanta, Lucy as she comes over tomorrow, and Shelton as he goes home tomorrow. I pray for the Crafts—be with them in a special way so that they might feel your presence. I love you, Lord, and thank you for this special time and all your blessing of this day. Lord, I'm tired tonight. You know my needs better than I do myself, so I humbly ask for your help.*

*Love,*
*Your child, Anne*

### Saturday February 26, 2005

*Thank you, Lord, for another wonderful day!!! Thank you for your protection last night when I fell. Once again you went before me, for Connie held me, and I didn't get hurt. Thank you for looking after me so well. I am indeed your child. I feel your love and protection all around me. I pray this treatment series has put my cancer into remission. I also ask for your favor regarding fever, infection, and mouth sores—Lord, let there be none. I praise you again for all your love and care. Please continue to bless me and use me to glorify you in all things.*

*Connie and Lucy have been here all day, and we have had so much fun. Shelton went home today so that he could preach tomorrow. I pray you will bless him with your wisdom as he preaches and use his message for your honor and glory. I pray Palmer and Holly will go to church tomorrow and that in your great wisdom, you will use all of these difficult trials for good in the lives of my family. I had two things of blood today and do feel much better. Give a special blessing to the people who gave that blood, for it is being used to help me heal.*

*Goodnight. See you in the morning.*

*Love you,*

*Anne*

### Sunday, February 27, 2005

*Thank you, Lord, so much for another good day and night. You are so wonderful. Thank you for all you do for me. You are life to me. I love you. I have such peace about my future because I know you are in control. I rejoice in knowing that I am your child whom you love. I commit this day to you and ask to be a reflection of you, showing love and compassion to those I come in contact with. Your grace and mercy abounds in my life's circumstances. There is no fever, no infection. Thank you, thank you, my loving Heavenly Father. Every day, I ask your blessing upon all the amazing doctors, nurses, and other health care providers who minister so tenderly and thoroughly to my physical needs. I believe you have directed me to this hospital and to Dr. Spitzer. I am in awe of all the ways you care for me. Thank you, precious Lord. I'll write more later.*

*Love,*

*Your child, Anne*

## Monday, February 28

*Heavenly Father,*

*I praise and thank you for another wonderful day in your presence. I have felt so well today and know it is a gift from you. Oh, how can I ever praise and thank you enough? You are in control of whatever happens to me, and I trust you for my week. I know, Lord, that seven days of chemo may not put this disease into remission, so I pray that you will prepare me for a bone marrow transplant if that is what you will for me. I pray for each one of my siblings, Sonny, John, and Ethel, as they have their bone marrow blood test. May at least one of them be a perfect match. But Lord, you are in control of that too, and I know you will work it out for your glory. Above all else, I want to glorify you and be a witness for you. Be glorified, Lord, through my proclamations of your control over my circumstances and your care in allowing whatever is best for me. I thank you for taking Connie safely back to Rock Hill and Shelton safely to and from Atlanta today. I just praise and thank you for who you are and how you are working in my life. Thank you for all those who are interceding in prayer for me!! I do pray for the Pendergrasses today—allow there to be a good report on the bone marrow test tomorrow. They need your encouragement.*

*Help me to follow you as a sheep follows the shepherd. Talk to you in the morning. I love you!!*

*Anne*

## Tuesday, March 1, 2005

*Hello, God,*

*My heart is full as I praise and thank you so much for another wonderful day. I am grateful that I have felt so well today and have had no fever. I don't take this for granted, for I know all these good things are because of your mercy imparted to me. I love you and so want to glorify you in all things. I come before you as a beggar, longing for your love, care, peace, kindness, goodness, greatness, and strength. You are indeed God; you know what I need and what is best for me. I rejoice that my white count was down today, and I pray it will be even less in the AM. I plead with you for healing—please let the bone marrow test I will have next week show that the cancer is in remission. This is my most fervent prayer. Perhaps I will only have to have two more chemo treatments. My life is in your hands. I do pray that Sonny, John, and Ethel will be a match for me should I need a bone marrow transplant. Oh please, Father, let this cancer be in remission so that I won't need a transplant. I had a great day with my precious Shelton here. I pray he will make it home safely tomorrow and that Connie will get here safely in the AM. I ask for your blessings and favor for the missions conference scheduled for Wednesday, for Richard Pratt as he preaches, and for all who participate. Let it be glorifying to you. I pray for a good, safe PM tonight and another blessed day tomorrow. I love you as I sign off for now. I rest in knowing though I have sinned against you, graciously you have forgiven me for all things!*

*In Jesus' name,*

*Anne, your child*

## Wednesday, March 2, 2005

*Today has been another wonderful day, and I praise and thank you for it. I had a fever, but they started antibiotics, and it went away immediately. Dr Spitzer said they are going to do a bone marrow test tomorrow. They will give me something for pain. I hope we will get the results from it soon. Sonny, John, and Ethel have sent their blood in, and I am praying one of them will be a match for me in case I need a bone marrow transplant. Connie came this AM, and Shelton went back for the beginning of the missions conference. Bless his heart, he came back last PM so he could be with me today. Thank you, Father, for loving me and giving me your peace through each step of the way. You give me the courage to do what I need to do. I realized today, Lord, that the leukemia is worse than I really thought, and it is going to be difficult to rid my body of this disease. Lord, I want to live so I can tell others about you. Please help me get well. I yearn to be with my family and to have a godly influence on them. I pray the missions conference will go well today and thank you for a good meeting last PM. I am so thankful you are my loving Heavenly Father. More later, but know how much I love you and want to serve you.*

*In Jesus' name,*
*Your child Anne*

## Friday, March 4, 2005

*I was out of it yesterday since I had a bone marrow test. They gave me morphine, Phenergan, and Benadryl, so I slept all day.*

## Saturday, March 5, 2005

*I feel great today! Two parts of the bone marrow report came back with good results! Dr Spitzer said he would not have to do another chemo this week. What an answer to prayer! Lucy is coming this afternoon, and Shelton is going back home. Heavenly Father, I cannot praise you enough for all you have given us and specifically how you have blessed me.*

### Sunday, March 6, 2005

*I'm getting caught up in my journal. On Saturday, a rash I have had for several days really got wild looking, so a dermatologist took a biopsy of three of them. Don't know when I will hear. The rash is on my back, my arms, and one leg. But thank you, Lord, it doesn't hurt or itch. I thank you too that I haven't had a bad fever and the low-grade ones have gone away with Tylenol. I pray that will continue to be the case. Lucy and I had a good day yesterday. (Sat) Connie went back to take Will to a birthday party. Shelton left about 2 o'clock to go back for the Saturday PM missions conference dinner and for the church services today. Barbara and Earl Lovelace stopped by yesterday afternoon and waved from the door as Lucy talked with them. I slept well in the PM. Before I went to bed, I had a bathroom accident next to my bed. I was laughing so hard at Lucy and Jewell I couldn't stop!!! It was embarrassing, but I couldn't help it. I don't get embarrassed much anymore. Lord, you are so near and dear to me. I thank you for being my Father and blessing me in so many ways. Without you, I couldn't stand this for a day. Yet Lord, I so want to be a good witness for you. Please give me the strength to meet the demands of each day and night. Thank you for giving me the strength to go through the pain. If I have a bone marrow test this week, I do ask that it not be as painful as the last one. I thank you, Lord, for your love and continued care. This is going to be a harder disease to beat than I had thought. I know that with your help, I can get over it and once again do the things I enjoy doing. I want to be able to give spoken testimony of your love and grace in my life so that others might come to know your joy, peace, patience, gentleness, love, kindness, self-control, goodness, and faithfulness. Today (Sunday) I have felt good thanks to you. Lucy has left to go home, and Connie is on her way here. Shelton will come back in the PM after church is over. Lucy took the scissors today and cut my hair real short all over my head. It feels so much better and doesn't look too bad. Precious Susan and Vickie sent me a beautiful wig that I am crazy about. Shelton and the girls think it looks very natural, and it is quite comfortable. I pray, Lord, that tomorrow will be a good news day. May the second part of the test come back with good results-- that one or more of my siblings will be a match for my bone marrow. You are an awesome God, and I love you so much. You have been with me thus far through all you have planned for me. I trust you with all aspects of my life. Thank you for giving me the best family in the world. I have gotten tired. Remember how much I love you and need you.*

*Love,*

*Your child Anne*

## Monday, March 7, 2005

*Heavenly Father,*

*I am thanking and praising you for who you are and how you have answered our prayers about the second part of the bone marrow test. You are such an awesome God, and I love you and trust you in all things. Thank you, thank you, thank you!! At midnight I had a fever of 102 degrees. After taking Tylenol, it went away. Thank you, Lord that my fevers have been low and Tylenol has taken care of them. Please let that continue. I thank you that I felt better this AM after my "little spell." I pray that it was just from weakness. Heavenly Father, I thank you for the peace and love you give me, and I praise your name for your power!! I pray, Lord, that I will get the pathology test about my rash back tomorrow and that it will be clear--with no cancer. I thank you that the two cultures came back negative, and I pray it will just dry up and go away as quickly as it came. I thank you in advance for what you are going to do about this rash. I also pray we will hear soon about the sibling bone marrow test and that at least one of my siblings will be a match. Please let us hear good news about that soon. Also, please let my body begin making good cells and let all of my counts that need to go up do so. I adore you and give you praise! Honor and glory be unto you alone! Thank you also for such a wonderful missions conference. You blessed it in so many ways, and I thank you for hearing and answering our prayers. Thank you, Lord, so much for everything. A cute story today– people have been so sweet to send me lots of cards and packages. Today when the mail lady brought my mail, she told me quite a number of people had been trying to figure out just who was getting all this mail from all over the world. Finally, they figured I must be Governor Mark Sanford's mother!! Shelton and I got a big laugh out of that!! I'll sign off from writing to you now. I feel your close presence, and I am confident you will give me the strength to get through this. I love you.*

   *Good night,*

   *Anne, your child*

## Tuesday, March 8, 2005

*Heavenly Father,*

   *I love you so much, and I am very appreciative of your love, guidance, and strength. This has been a delightful day as we have gotten good reports on the rash biopsy—it's an inflammation and not cancer. I thank you for that. Then Dr. Spitzer came by to inform us none of my siblings are a match.*

*He will not do the bone marrow transfer now. I had prayed for one of my siblings to be a match, and I know, Lord, if you had wanted me to have the bone marrow transfer, one of them would have matched. I commit that to you, believing you know what is best for me. Dr. Spitzer plans to start reducing my antibiotics to see if my new immunities will kick in. My main prayer requests at present are that my counts will go up, I won't have any fever or infection, and I will be able to go home on Saturday for a few days. I pray the bone marrow biopsy will not hurt. Many people came by today to see my rash. No one really knows what it is. I thank you for your care, love, control over every creature, peace, joy, and all that I experience in you. You are an awesome God, and I am so glad that you are my guide, directing me in every way. Good night for now!!! I thank you!!!*

*Love,*

*Anne, your child.*

For the next few days, Anne's fever continued on and off. But on March 10, Anne's blood count had recovered to a level that was even better than when she was first diagnosed.

Dr. Spitzer stopped by her room that morning and said, "Well hello, Ms. Delightful, how are you feeling today?"

With a smile so bright that it would make sunshine envious, Anne replied, "I am as good as the Lord Jesus would wish me to feel. In other words, I am feeling great! With the Lord as my Shepherd on this path, how can I feel otherwise?"

"Well then, on that note, I have both good news and bad news for you. Where do I start?" Gary asked.

"Dr. Spitzer, no news is ever bad news for me. I just told you, ever since I asked Jesus to help me sail through this trial, no news is ever going to be bad news for me. But, if you insist, start with the news you think is bad."

He replied, "The bad news is that you will need to undergo another bone marrow test later today. The good news is that your blood count has improved so well that today you are healthier than you were the first time you saw Dr. Patel! I'm sure your bone marrow test is going to have good results. And don't worry about the pain; I will make sure that we give you enough morphine and Benadryl for you to not feel a thing! After we have the results, I do believe that we may even be able to send you home for a few days!"

With noticeable relief, Anne said, "I'm quite ready for a break, Dr. Spitzer. Thanks for your kind words. I have lots of things to do at home. I really had no idea how intensive this process was going to be when it first began. I have to write thank you notes to all the people praying for me across the world. And I also have to spend lots of time thanking the Lord for his guidance throughout this process."

She was ready to go home. This was the first time since moving to Rock Hill that she had ever been away from her home for so long.

The bone marrow test was uneventful. Anne was so involved in the thought of going home and catching up with her activities that she barely noticed the needle entering or leaving her bone marrow cavity. She simply kept on praying to the Lord for any residual leukemia to be cleared so that she could go home and regain her normal life.

Soon after the test results had been analyzed, Dr. Spitzer arrived with a smile on his face. Shelton and Connie were also in the room.

"Anne, I have very good news," Dr. Spitzer began.

"Can I go home today?" she anxiously asked. In spite of all of her patience, perseverance, and faith, she was experiencing a touch of impatience and anxiety.

"I have even better news than that. Your blood count has normalized completely. And your leukemia is in remission. Are you happy now?" Gary replied, the ever-widening smile on his face telling all.

Tears of joy started rolling from everyone's eyes. Shelton and Connie had already helped Anne pack up her things to go home. There had been an unspoken shadow in everyone's mind. Perhaps the bone marrow test would reveal something unpleasant, and their return home would not be possible. Until that moment, they had no idea whether they would be able to go home or how long they would be there. For the first time in a month, they saw the light at the end of the tunnel.

Anne could feel a bright light shining on her. It was as if she was being lifted up in the air on the broad hands of the Lord's angels to receive blessings.

# CHAPTER 4
# LIFE
# RETURNS

*We are never far from where we need to be.*
*God would not have brought us to this place in our life,*
*if He didn't have something for us to receive.*
—DALE FINCH

NO ONE QUITE KNEW HOW to react to the news. This was too good to be true. All of their prayers had just been answered. It took a few minutes for them to digest everything.

Of late, Shelton's life had come to a screeching halt. He had lost his direction. In spite of all of his faith and trust in Jesus Christ, he was vulnerable to the same fears that any ordinary human being would face in his position. Although his faith in Almighty God was never in question, there were days when he was not sure what the future would hold for them.

Now, he was sure once again. For the first time, his family managed to come out of the darkness that leukemia had pulled them into, and they were able to start planning their lives anew. One thing all of them, especially Anne, had realized was that any day in life could be their last day, and from now on they resolved to resume life with that in mind.

Connie was the first to speak. "What's next, Dr. Spitzer? Where do we go from here? Can we take some more time off and let Mom rest?"

"I really don't want to reinforce Dr. Patel's belief that I am a pessimist," Dr. Spitzer replied, "but I think we still need to be on guard. Leukemia is the last disease you ever want to take lightly. My gray hairs and wrinkles have come early after seeing far too many unpleasant surprises, so I am not one to prematurely rejoice. This type of leukemia is particularly unpredictable; it could well be hiding and come back with a vengeance at a later date. After ten days at home, I think that Anne should come back to the hospital for another week of treatment."

It was as if a rain cloud suddenly covered their short-lived sunshine. For a moment, Anne, Shelton, and Connie had forgotten about leukemia. They hoped that they could relax a bit and put thoughts of leukemia out of their minds for a time. Now, there remained a niggling doubt—was it actually gone or just hiding? Anne had secretly nursed a hope that she would not have to come back to the hospital. For a glorious five minutes, all thoughts of leukemia had left their minds. They only wished Dr. Spitzer had withheld the discussion of the cancer coming back for at least a few days.

And yet, Anne was the least bothered of them all. At that point, she counted it as a victory simply to go back home and sleep in her own bed that night. She had never envisioned that she would be away from home for more than a month. She wanted to look through her window and see the gorgeous dogwood tree in her backyard and the azaleas that reminded her of her first truly romantic meeting with Shelton. She longed for the smell of fresh gardenias and pines. No amount of pessimism on Dr. Spitzer's behalf would squash the wonderful joy she felt at being able to return home.

The treatment had left Anne exhausted. Her hair was rapidly thinning and falling out. Although Lucy had done a good job trimming the hair that remained, Anne's scalp was still visible. Her skin had started exhibiting premature wrinkles from the chemotherapy. Her physical strength had weakened. She was experiencing deconditioning, a medical disorder that usually affects individuals who have to stay in hospitals for long periods of time.

Without any further discussions of leukemia returning, she had resolved to finally make her way back home. As soon as she stepped out of bed, she began trembling. She suddenly realized just how weak she had become, and despite clinging to Connie and Shelton's arms, the short walk through the parking lot to their car felt like a marathon. Although she was still near one hundred percent mentally, physically the leukemia and the chemotherapy poisons had taken their toll. They had to stop three times to let Anne catch her breath before they made it to the car.

A surprise was waiting for her at home. Connie and Lucy had decorated the house for Anne's homecoming. All the rooms were filled with balloons, flowers, and cards from well wishers. She felt like a newlywed entering her husband's house for the first time. Tears of joy poured down her cheeks. Exhausted from the two-hour car drive, she went to her room to sleep. Her bed was every bit as comfortable as she remembered.

The day of her return home was exactly one month after the day of her leukemia diagnosis. Like that first day, the sky was blue, and not a single cloud blocked the warmth of the sun's rays. As soon as she woke up, Anne went straight to her favorite spot on the deck. Spring was early. Birds had already nested on the dogwood branches. White petals were slowly creeping through their green stems to welcome the arrival of the season, and pink and red azaleas were already beginning to bloom. Anne put the Beatles on her CD player.

*Yesterday ... all my troubles seemed so far away.....*

As John Lennon sang, she slipped into her distant past, cherishing the best moments in her life. She remembered the day that Shelton proposed. She started drifting into a past full of fun, romance, and enjoyment... a place where troubles seemed far away.

*Now it seems as though they're here to stay....*

As the lyrics continued, she began thinking about the present again—a present that was uncharted, unpredictable, and uncertain. Her own illness wasn't her main worry; rather, it was the effect it was having on Shelton. His love for her knew no bounds. Although he was suffering terribly, she knew he wanted to hide it from her to prevent her from worrying. She knew that if anything were to happen to her, Shelton would find it extremely difficult to move on.

*Now I need a place to hide away ...*

Although outwardly she revealed nothing but full optimism, in the depths of her soul Anne felt that perhaps death was on the horizon. In between Dr. Spitzer's words, she had read a genuine fear that the leukemia was more likely than not to come back. She began to prepare herself in case of that eventuality, and those preparations were changing her view on life. Now more than ever she could see divinity everywhere. In each and every form of creation around her, she saw the presence and glory of God. In the song of the mockingbirds surrounding her, in the white buds of the dogwood, and in the fragrant scent of pine wafting through the lush backyard, she could see the wonders of the hands of the Almighty. Only the will of the Living God could create such a wonderful world. If he had the power to create a world this beautiful, she was sure that nothing he did was wrong. Even if her struggle against leukemia ended in her death, she knew that the warm, guiding hand of the Lord was with her for eternity. She had found her place to hide away: it was in the healing arms of her Sovereign Protector.

Her thoughts were broken by the soft voice of Connie over the lyrics of John Lennon. "Mom, dinner is ready. I know you love sitting here when you're full of thoughts, but you still need to eat and be strong. There will be another round of treatment soon, and we have to keep you well nourished."

Connie's voice gently reminded Anne of the worldly commitments and duties she still had to perform. The fight was not over yet; while she may have accepted the possibility that her battle would end in her death, that possibility was no reason for her to stop fighting.

Connie's voice also reminded her of something else that saddened her. It reminded Anne that her role was changing from helper and caregiver to someone who needed help and care. This also reminded her that perhaps her time was limited and that she needed to start prioritizing what she should do in the time she had left.

Suddenly she stopped herself. "No, this isn't true. Why am I getting these depressing ideas and thoughts? I am going to beat this. I am already in remission. While I may be able to accept that I might lose, it would be an insult to God if I were to stop fighting and give up all together. He has still given me the strength to walk and be with my family at home, and he has also given me the strength to continue treatment. I am not giving up the fight. Didn't Dr. Spitzer say I was even better today than when I was first diagnosed?" Anne began teetering between optimism and pessimism. Accepting the possibility of death was quite different from accepting that death was the only possibility, and Anne knew that she still had some strength to keep fighting.

Her silent debate was beginning to worry Connie. "Mom! Are you okay? Did you hear me?"

"Oh yes! I am so sorry, Connie! I heard you. It's just so pleasant here that I forget about my surroundings and lose track of time. I'm coming, honey."

She slowly stood from her favorite chair on the deck and began taking small but firm steps towards the dining room.

As she saw all the flowers, cards, and balloons inside, Anne once again thought that perhaps from this point on she was going to be on the receiving end of acts of kindness from family, friends, and the community. Until this time, she had devoted her whole life to helping and serving others in need. Now, it was her name on the prayer lists of hundreds of churches around the world. Every single day she was getting messages and prayers offering hope and spiritual help for her fight against the deadly leukemia. What the Scriptures teach about doing unto others as you would have them do unto you was true. She had always felt it was important to do good for others; now others were doing nothing but good for her.

As she walked up to the dining table, she noticed that something was different. The house was still the same, and she couldn't quite put her finger on the difference. Suddenly, it hit her. The entire table had been rearranged, beginning from the layout of plates and silverware to where the serving bowls were placed. Although it did not particularly bother her, she had been so meticulous throughout her life that even such a minute change made itself obvious.

Noticing her hesitation to take the chair, Connie asked, "Mom, do you need any help? You seem weak and unsteady. Let me hold your hands and help you to the table."

"I'm okay, Connie. It's just that … the table looks so different. This leukemia has even changed some of the smallest things in my life. I can walk by myself to the table. By the way, where am I sitting?" Anne responded.

"On your usual chair! Right next to Dad's chair!" Connie replied, somewhat perplexed. "You've always sat there."

They all sat down at the table to share what used to be a weekly gathering for them. Shelton was there, along with Connie and her son Will. Lucy and Palmer, her two other children, were also there, accompanied by their spouses and Lucy's daughter Burns.

It was Anne's first meal at home after a month-long stay in the hospital, and she was ready to enjoy it. The leukemia was gone from her body, at least temporarily, and her loved ones surrounded her. It was time to enjoy life with her family. Shelton thanked the Lord for the wonderful day and the dinner, and he asked the Lord's blessings for Anne and the rest of the family.

*Lord Jesus,*

*On this wonderful day, we are so grateful for your tender mercies and loving care.*

*Thank you for bringing Anne home to be with us. We are so thankful for your saving grace and your great love for our family. May this meal you have graciously provided bring nourishment to our bodies.*

*In Jesus' name, amen!*

Everyone was rejoicing that they were all together again, except Anne. Although she was very happy and felt truly blessed for being in remission, she knew there was still a long way to go. She was keenly aware leukemia could change all equations in a fraction of a second. Her body had been physically wrecked in the battle between the cancerous cells and the normal cells aided by chemotherapy poisons, and her otherwise healthy tissues suffered as collateral damage. Before becoming melancholic, she decided to focus on the positive and all the good things that she had going for her. She was at home with her family, enjoying a meal with her husband at her side. She smiled, and the thoughts of the leukemia faded into the background.

When they went to bed that evening, Shelton told her how excited he was about the good results from the bone marrow test. He hugged Anne and once again thanked God for the positive step in their fight against cancer. For the first time in a month, he was able to fall asleep instantly. The previous month had been filled with stressful and sleepless nights; his daytime job as a senior pastor supporting his flock and his nighttime job of supporting Anne in her struggle against leukemia left him with little time to relax.

Anne closed her eyes and pretended to fall asleep. She could not understand why even her favorite pillow felt odd to her. With a start, she realized her hair loss had exposed her scalp, and she had never known the feeling of her own pillow on hairless skin. Although everyone else thought that life was finally getting back to normal, for Anne everything had changed, perhaps forever. Her own pillow felt unfamiliar to her. Her hair, the table, indeed, the entire house, seemed changed. Although her family was the same, she experienced the sense that she was losing control, and that made it difficult for her to accept things as they were. No, she wasn't a control freak by nature. Perhaps she was going through an adjustment phase in her life again. Every phase of life was temporary and subject to change. Suddenly, she realized that her own stay in the world was included in that. Once again she went into a cycle of optimism and pessimism. Dr. Spitzer told her that if she made it through fifty-nine more months without the leukemia coming back, she would be declared safe.

The thoughts slowly faded away as she finally fell asleep. Tonight would be the first night in a month that no nurse or ward staff would wake her up in the middle of the night to check her blood pressure or other vitals.

She awakened the next morning refreshed and relaxed, although she still felt weak. Connie already had breakfast ready. After quickly eating, Anne went to visit her friends at Piedmont hospital and her church. Everyone was pleasantly surprised at her arrival. Although visibly weak, leukemia had failed to dampen her perennial smile or her desire to continue bringing happiness and blessings to every soul that she came in contact with.

The week went by without many changes to note. Each day she spent at home was doing wonders for her, and she kept feeling stronger and stronger. She had an appointment at my office on March 19 for a blood check. This test would be able to determine the recovery of her blood count—an important factor in her overall recovery. She arrived at noon.

April, one of my medical office assistants, drew her blood and ran it through a blood analyzer. While still waiting for the results to come through, I started talking to Anne.

"Anne, I know a lot of things have changed for you in the last month. I have dealt with leukemia for over a decade in my career, and I know that it changes so many things for the patient. I'm sure you must be trying to adapt to changes right now."

"Yes, Dr. Patel," Anne replied. "The most difficult part is losing my independence. I always thought that I'd be the one helping others, especially Shelton and my children. It seems that the Lord is testing my patience and faith by giving me this leukemia. On the other hand, I'm glad that Almighty God chose me in place of another for this test since I have enough love and support to not be alone in my fight." No matter what, her faith was undeterred.

"I understand your feelings very well, Anne," I said. "You've always given everything to your family. You have lived your life in a way that would help others have a better life. Your work at the hospital has helped countless needy souls during the worst times of their lives. You even helped my young son who was hopelessly lost on his first day of volunteering there. To this day, he still remembers you and the kindness you showed. I can imagine how distressing it must be to you to have to hold onto someone else's hands now."

I wanted to reassure her that there was nothing wrong with accepting the assistance of others to help her through her fight. I also wanted to offer reassurance regarding the potential of the cancer returning; I knew that Dr. Spitzer had probably painted the worst-case scenario and left it at that.

"It's not the fear of losing my independence that really scares me. It's that I may never be able to serve people again!" Anne's philanthropic soul was again visibly shaken. "Can I ask you a personal question, Dr. Patel?" she asked shyly.

"By all means! Please don't worry; you can ask me anything, Anne," I assured her, wanting to reinforce the fact that she could always be frank with me without fear.

"I was wondering what type of religious sect or faith you belong to. I know you're from India originally. When you speak, I hear the influence of Christianity in your words. You don't have to answer if you don't feel comfortable with sharing. I was just curious," Anne reluctantly said.

There was a brief moment of silence that Anne misinterpreted. "I didn't mean to offend you. Please, don't answer if you don't feel like it. I shouldn't have asked such a personal question," Anne continued, visibly shaken.

"No, no, it isn't that. It's just that I find it a difficult question for me to answer, and none of my patients have asked me this before. I was thinking how to best explain my beliefs to you," I responded. "I'm not a man who's overly fixated on religion. By birth I am Hindu, but Hindu scholars maintain that Hinduism is a way of life—one not marked by any specific rites or rituals. I was educated for twelve years by Jesuits in a Catholic school, and some of my best friends are Muslim. My family has always been secular. My son even went to a Catholic school when we lived in England. I moved around so much before coming to the Carolinas that I never really identified with a certain religion or identity."

I paused briefly before continuing. "To be honest, I don't follow any specific ritual or faith that could be considered a religion. Although I may not be religious, I am very spiritual. To answer your question, my beliefs are mostly in line with the secular spirituality that Mahatma Gandhi taught and advocated."

Anne then spoke. "That is interesting. I was right—you do have some understanding of Christianity's teachings. It seems that you represent the cultural, ethnic, and religious melting pot they say the United States is regarded as. Your patients are truly blessed to have you as their physician. I hope that you won't mind telling me more about this religious secularism you said Gandhi taught and you follow. Where do you learn how to enhance your faith? How do you perform religious practices? "

"I'll try my best to summarize for you," I responded. "Let me answer your last question first. I rarely go to formal places of worship like shrines or temples. This isn't because I have something against organized worship, but because I think that God is everywhere. I believe he is in the trees and the birds of my backyard as much as he is in the idols inside temples. He is in the rivers and the oceans as much as he is in churches and synagogues. I see the hand of God in everything, even in the smile of my wife and son and in the face of everyone who walks through my doors. Every single patient who comes into my office is one of God's children. Knowing this, I offer the very best of my services for each and every one of them, for in their way, they are each a different manifestation of the Creator. I believe it is the duty of every person to serve God's creations to the fullest of his or her abilities. You see, to some degree, my work is my worship. I don't have to go to a temple to pray; rather, my prayer is in my service to all I encounter. Aren't all of us children of God? If so, my time is better served here, in my office, treating people and making their lives better. To me, all religions are just different paths to the same end. Just like all rivers eventually meet the ocean, so too do all religions eventually meet the same spirituality that I try to implement in my life. I will be honest; there have been times when I have not been able to follow my ideals. There are times when I am prone to judging people. Nevertheless, such failures are less and less the longer I stay in practice."

"You mean to say that you never go to places of worship at all? That sounds strange!" Anne wondered aloud.

"I do occasionally go to Hindu temples. But I do not go as much as most people do. There is one Hindu prayer that I am especially fond of reciting, and it happens to also have been Gandhi's favorite prayer. Its main line is 'Ishwar, Allah tero naam. Sab ko samati de Bhagavan.' This translates to 'Ishwar or Allah, whatever be your name, we consider you God.' Ishwar is the generic name for God in Hinduism, and Allah is the name of God in Islam."

I was getting more engaged in this conversation, not realizing that I was exploring my own conscience deeper and deeper.

I continued. "Although I did have some formal religious education in Hinduism and Christianity, most of my spiritual learning in life actually came from Mahatma Gandhi. My father, when he was a child, had the privilege of seeing Gandhi in person and always followed his ideologies throughout his life. Every weekend he would take me to Mahatma Gandhi's ashram, which was in my hometown, and would make me read episodes about the simplicity of his way of life. Memories of Gandhi's life stories helped shape my own religious building blocks from what I learned of Hinduism, Christianity, and Islam. While in America, I became friends with one of the descendents from Gandhi's family and heard first-hand accounts of his life and message. And finally, I learned from patients and individuals like you. Having lived in three different continents and seven different metropolitan areas, from New York to Manchester to Mumbai, I have met all sorts of people—various and different images of the children of God–and learned a lot simply by observing and engaging in heart-to-heart conversations with them."

"Amazing! You just said you have lived in Manchester and in Mumbai? Tell me more! I'm becoming more curious about you by the minute. Did you do the same thing that you are doing here? I mean, did you run an oncology clinic?" Anne eagerly asked.

"No, in that chapter of my life I was doing something quite different. To be brief, I didn't work as an oncologist. I was undergoing training to be a hematologist in Great Britain," I summarized.

"That means you had to have trained again here in the US? Connie told me you were trained in New York and Philadelphia… hmmm. Did you not get tired and bored of repeating your training?" Anne asked.

"As matter of fact, I have undergone residency three times: once in India, again in the UK, and yet again in the US. But no, I never got bored!" I replied.

"And why is that? Did you think retraining was necessary?"

"No, it wasn't that. I didn't think retraining was necessary, but I didn't have a choice. To practice in any country, you have to do your residency there. But the reason I never got bored was that I saw it as an opportunity to rectify mistakes I had made in the past. Every time I repeated residency, I learned more and more about how to avoid mistakes that I committed previously. Not to brag, but if I was to do it a fourth time, I think I would be a near-perfect resident doctor! My dad always taught me to look at something like repeating residency as another opportunity to learn and perfect my skills as a physician rather than cursing the additional challenge and negative change of life it would inevitably bring. There were some times in the beginning when I felt exhausted and thought I was wasting my time. But as time went on, such thoughts invariably diminished."

"Wow, Dr. Patel, you really are a lot different from most of the doctors I've seen. I feel like this conversation could last forever! But I'm sure you have many more patients to still see," Anne said. "Maybe we can continue this conversation sometime in the future."

"Don't worry about time limits in conversations with me, Anne. Did you notice that there isn't a single clock in this room and that I don't wear a wristwatch? There is a reason for both. When I am with any patient, I want to devote my heart, mind, and soul to putting that person at ease, regardless of how long that takes. Sometimes this results in patients having to wait while I finish up with others, but they all know my style of practice and don't mind it. They know that whenever their turn comes, they will have one hundred percent of my time and attention. How can I cut short any encounter with a fellow creation of God?" I said in response.

"I must say, Dr. Patel, I do enjoy talking to you. You are unique. Do you ever find yourself out of place in this culture? It seems that everyone nowadays is short on time and is running around everywhere trying to make up for it. They've all forgotten about spending time with the people they care about, and they sacrifice time with their families so that they'll never be classified as tardy," Anne said. My attitude towards time really surprised her.

"Do I feel out of place? Well, yes and no. When I was in residency and fellowship working for a hospital, I couldn't adopt such a style of work. But now that I run my own practice, I can treat patients in the manner I think best fits them. I have to share a small episode from my personal life with you so that you can understand why I have never encountered a stranger or felt out of place during my life."

This is the story I shared with Anne Sanford.

Almost thirty years ago, I was traveling in a remote tribal place in India with my dad, who was one of the foremost construction engineers working for the state government. He was involved in developing roads and bridges. We were in a rugged four-wheel drive that was at least ten years old. It was a hot Indian summer day. I was sitting in the front with the chauffeur. We heard a strange whizzing sound from the engine. The radiator had started leaking from a small, rusted hole. The driver pulled out a bar of cheap bathing soap and smeared the hole, hoping that it would last until we reached a repair shop. The whizzing continued, although it was less intense, and the driver periodically reapplied the soap.

A few miles later we came across large leaves on the road. All of a sudden the car began reeling back and forth. It turned out that one of the leaves had a large nail underneath it, and it punctured the rear tire. Nomadic people living in that area used to hide large nails on the road to cause tire bursts so they could loot and rob stranded travelers. There we were, on a lonely jungle road, in a car with a burst tire and a radiator held together with soapsuds. The driver nervously left the car and changed the tire, looking over his shoulder the entire time. He finally finished, and we kept going, entering a thick jungle that was known for its population of wild bears. While the others were busy discussing and looking for telltale signs of bears, I was extremely nervous and worried.

My father noticed my anxiety and asked, "Son, what is bothering you?" Being embarrassed, I said that nothing was bothering me. He knew that something was wrong though, so he asked again, "You look worried. Are you scared?"

I acquiesced and said, "Yes, Dad, I'm scared. We're so far away from civilization in this jungle, and no one knows if tribal robbers will come and rob us or if a bear will come and attack us. We have nothing to protect us at all."

My father responded, "Son, we are never far from help. The Earth has given us its fruits and sustained us like a loving mother. No matter where we are, we are always in the lap of mother earth. Why should we ever be scared in the lap of our mother? You are at home in every part of this world, no matter how strange or scary some parts may seem; it is all part of the nourishing whole that has supplied us with life. The Almighty always watches over his creations constantly and will look after us in whatever corner of the world we may be in."

This wasn't too convincing to my scared mind. I replied, "That's all well and good, but I see no one nearby. Literally or figuratively, I don't see how we are safe here like we are at home."

My father then said, "No, son, what I am saying is absolutely true and supported by geometry. You just need to apply the broader context of knowledge. It is all about perspective."

This made no sense to me, so I asked, "What do you mean?"

"Is Earth a sphere?" he asked me.

"Yes," I replied.

"So any point on it can be considered the center of its surface perimeter?" he asked.

"Yes. But I don't see how geometry in any way offers protection from robbers or bears," I replied.

"I am not done explaining yet," he continued. "What is the most important thing a mother does for her child after giving birth?"

"Feeds it with her own milk, I believe—nurtures him or her."

"Yes, son, you are getting it. Now then, where do you get your food from?" he asked.

I replied, "From the fruit and vegetable market!"

"No, that is where you buy it from. Where did those fruits and vegetables grow?"

"Soil?" I replied.

"Yes. Now then, is soil a part of perimeter of this Earth? Both literally and figuratively?" he continued. "Is it true that is the soil of the Earth feeds you for your entire life—even longer than your own mother? Is this not nature's maternal instinct?"

"You can say so," I replied.

"Isn't it true then that right now you are in the center of the lap of your mother? Someone who has fed you selflessly for much longer than your own biological mother?" he asked.

"Yes, it is true. But why would she care about me? She has to feed everyone on this planet," I replied.

"Why should that matter? No loving mother would leave any of her children hungry, no matter if she had two, five, or even ten. All her children hold an equal place in her heart. Similarly, mother earth sustains life for all living beings. So she will protect and look after you wherever and whenever she can. In every place in the world, people are made of and fed by the same soil of mother earth. You should never feel unsafe anywhere on this planet. That is precisely why I have never felt scared in my life."

As I finished my story, I told Anne, "Ever since I had that conversation with my father, I have never been afraid of any unfamiliar place in the world. I came to England with a hundred pounds in my pocket and no idea where I was going to live. Even then I wasn't scared, because I knew that no matter what, God and mother earth would look after me."

Anne listened to my story almost transfixed. I could see a tear running down her cheek.

"You really have a treasure of amazing life experiences, Dr. Patel. I think there's a lot I can learn from you, and maybe I can even teach you a thing or two!"

At that exact moment, April brought back Anne's blood test. I could tell from her smile that the news was good. I glanced at the results briefly and also smiled in turn. The results confirmed that for now all of her leukemia had been considered destroyed. The first hurdle had been passed. I told Anne the good news and added that she could well be looking forward to a healthy recovery.

"Well, now that your blood count has almost normalized, Anne, I may not need to see you until Dr. Spitzer administers another cycle of chemotherapy. Of course, I'll be here for any questions or concerns you may have. But I think that there are probably a thousand things you would like to be doing, and you're free to do so!"

Anne's face was suddenly filled with tears of joy. She couldn't hold back her excitement. "Does this mean that I am cured?"

"I'm afraid that's not quite right. You are in remission, and at the moment there isn't any leukemia in your blood. But leukemia can still come back during a window of the next five years. After that, most oncologists will officially declare you cured. However, from my personal experience, if the leukemia doesn't relapse in the next three or four years, I think we can safely say that you have been cured. In fact, as each year of remission passes, the chances of the leukemia coming back become less and less."

"Thank you, Dr. Patel! This is great! I always like your optimistic approach. And thank you for being so open and transparent with me!"

But then she suddenly paused. She placed her hand on the back of her head. She was almost completely bald. I could sense the disappointment and impatience she was feeling. She didn't need to express it in words.

"Anne, I can understand why you are bothered about losing your beautiful hair. Now that chemotherapy is over, it will definitely grow back. The beginning phases of recovery are the hardest, but like a phoenix rises from the ashes, so too will your body. The sky is always darkest just before dawn breaks, and trust me, it will soon break for you and your family. In the near future, maybe you can even join your husband on his trip to Taiwan and India and wear a saffron robe like the Dalai Lama!"

"Your analogies are wonderful, Dr. Patel. They put me at ease and also help me look at everything through a different perspective," she said, slightly recovered from her brief melancholy.

"Believe me, Anne, I'm not just saying these things to put your mind at ease. I truly mean everything I say. I have weathered many storms of different magnitudes. Just look at my hair! I am forty-three years old. I used to have thick, jet-black hair. Now it has turned to a salt and pepper look—with a lot more salt than pepper. Each grey hair is evidence of rough times I have been through. Although I stopped recalling and counting such harsh memories a long time ago, they are still there to remind me of consequences whenever I lose my sense of discretion and dedication to patients and to direct me to my purpose in life—to serve my patients. Like I said before, there is always something good that emanates out of tragedies. It's just that most of us aren't aware of it at that moment."

I wanted to reassure her that I wasn't just speaking empty words to comfort her. I meant everything I said.

"I can never stop wondering what you'll be telling me next, Dr. Patel. We should have another conversation soon."

"Now that you have regained your spirit and composure, I think I can safely let you stay home for the next few weeks before Gary begins his next round of treatments."

"Thank you, Dr. Patel. I think I've taken up quite enough of your time today. Although I feel like continuing this conversation forever, I need to let you go back to your other patients. We can pick up where we left off next time!"

She went home with the understanding that she would not be seeing me for another month or so, and she would have her next round of chemotherapy in Greenville very soon.

What would have been a fifteen minute test ended up lasting almost an hour. Fortunately, since it was a half-day for me and she was the last patient on schedule, no patients were left waiting.

The rest of the day went quite easily for Anne. Despite Connie's insistence that Anne rest and allow her to do the cooking, Anne made her way to the kitchen and prepared a wonderful meal for her family. This was the first sign that Anne was getting back to her routine. Many such days went by, and spring grew brighter and warmer. The birds began their melodies, and new leaves sprung from dry, barren stems at the same time that Anne's body began regaining and regenerating the cells and tissues that it had lost. The days and the weeks went by as leukemia left the minds of the whole family. Unfortunately, reality caught up with Anne on April 24 when she received an unwelcome phone call from St. Francis Hospital in Greenville.

# CHAPTER 5

# THE BATTLE INTENSIFIES

*The strongest oak of the forest*
*is not the one that is protected from the storm and hidden from the sun.*
*It's the one that stands in the open*
*where it is compelled to struggle for its existence*
*against the winds and rains and the scorching sun.*
—Napoleon Hill

"Hello, Ms. Sanford, this is Mary from St. Francis Hospital. Dr. Spitzer has asked me to relay that tomorrow we will have a special room ready for you on the sixth floor at the hospital for your treatment. We hope that your stay with us will be as pleasant as possible."

"Okay, I will be there. Can you make sure that I have the same room as before–the one with the beautiful view outside? It was facing the garden next to the parking lot." Anne was tired of strange hospital beds. She had gotten used to her old one and didn't want to adjust again.

"I will do my best," Mary promised before hanging up.

On April 25, the family made the second trip into Greenville. By now Anne was familiar with the semantics of being hospitalized. She went straight to the registration desk. The admissions clerk had already received information regarding her admission and room assignment. Anne showed her driver's license for verification purposes and was asked to sign papers indicating that she was responsible for non-covered expenses. An identity badge was applied to her wrist, and she was wheeled upstairs to the sixth floor. Mary had made good on her promise; Anne was given the same room that she was in during her stay in February.

She undressed and put on a hospital gown and in the process had to remove the beautiful wig her friends from Mississippi had bought for her. Once again, her independence was snatched away, and she had to start living by the instructions of hospital staff.

Gary Spitzer and Wendy came by at the end of the day. His manner of dress was even more unusual than anything she had previously seen—with his red socks, purple tie, and green overcoat, he looked more like a mad scientist pulled out of an experiment on time travel than he did an oncologist.

"Hello, young lady!" he began in his inimitable Australian accent. "It is so good to see you again! I'm sure Kashyap has briefly discussed remission and the reasoning behind the treatment that we plan on administering from now on. This treatment is going to be different than before and in all likelihood won't have nearly as many side effects as the last one."

He continued. "This is a consolidation treatment called HIDAC. HIDAC stands for high dose Ara-C. We will administer cytarabine, a chemotherapy drug, in a very high dose with the hope of eliminating any leukemia hiding in sanctuary sites like the brain, ovaries, or bone marrow. We will then harvest stem cells from your blood to perform an autologous bone marrow transplantation. Since this treatment is definitely different from the one before, I do not believe you will be half as sick, nor will you have the possibility of adverse side effects on your heart. However, in a small number of patients, this treatment can cause swelling of the cornea and brain—conditions called cerebritis and dry keratitis."

"Can you explain it a bit clearer, Dr. Spitzer? What will I feel if this happens?" she asked, wanting to know ahead of time what the worst possibilities could be.

"Well, Anne, it affects everyone differently. Some people may not notice symptoms. Others may become confused or get severe headaches. A very small percent of them may start developing seizures. If that happens, we will discontinue the medicine. And to prevent the possibility of dry keratitis, I will give you steroid eye drops. But hopefully you won't suffer any of these reactions," Dr. Spitzer explained honestly.

It was Connie's turn to ask questions. "How long will the infusions last? Will she get any nausea medications? How many doses will she need?"

Dr. Spitzer patiently replied, "She will receive this chemotherapy twice per day on alternate days for a total of six doses. As soon as she is done with her fifth day, we will send her home, and Dr. Patel will arrange for her to have white blood cell booster shots until her count recovers. That is when we will harvest stem cells for the autologous bone marrow transplant. I'll leave Wendy to explain everything in minute detail to you folks. I can assure you of one thing: Anne will not have nearly as rough a time as she had before."

After explaining that, Dr. Spitzer moved on to his next patient. Wendy then described the treatment plans in detail.

"Like before, we will check your blood to make sure that your liver and kidneys are in good enough shape to deal with the stress of such a large dose of chemotherapy. Then, you will receive an infusion of anti-nausea medication and steroids for thirty minutes each. These infusions will prevent any immediate side effects. After you receive those two drugs, we will start the chemotherapy. You will get it six times in concentrated form over two hours each, with the aim of clearing every nook and cranny of your body from any residual leukemia cells. Since the concentration and dose of cytarabine is so large, we will give you a break of thirty-six hours before beginning the next dose. Provided you don't develop any serious side effects after completing a total of six doses, we will let you go home."

"I'm concerned about the brain swelling and corneal dryness possibilities that Dr. Spitzer mentioned. Should there be any other side effects to look out for?" Connie asked.

"Well, do understand that those two are rare and uncommon side effects. Dr. Spitzer mentioned them because they are the most serious potential consequences. But very few of the people who get this treatment develop these side effects. Plus, we will take all the precautions we can to prevent them. We will administer steroids prior to infusion of these medications, and we will also be giving Anne prednisone eye drops to prevent complications. And finally, we will give her antibiotics to prevent any opportunistic infections."

"Thank God!" Connie replied, sounding relieved.

"Once she is done with infusion on the fifth day, we will send her back to Dr. Patel to start her on shots to boost her white blood cells. In turn, Dr. Patel will stay in touch with us about her daily blood count, and once her blood cells reach a certain threshold level, we will harvest her stem cells," Wendy elaborated.

"Thank you for explaining it so well, Wendy! I know that the Lord is once again going to lead me through this journey safe and sound," Anne said, her voice full of confidence. She knew that the Lord was her Shepherd. Whatever path and whichever destination he led her to, she would follow.

That evening was very busy. Different nurses and nursing assistants filtered in and out of Anne's room. Her body was checked from head to toe. A new electrocardiogram was taken to ensure that her heart was still able to withstand the side effects of chemotherapy. A phlebotomist came in and drew almost ten vials of blood. Anne thought that it was no wonder patients developed anemia so often in hospitals. If they kept checking blood like that two or three times a day, a patient would lose almost a pint of blood in a week's time!

While the hospital staff was busy finishing up all their tests in preparation for Anne's chemo the next morning, she was developing a strange sense of déjà vu. Everything seemed so familiar this time. She could see the same landscape outside her windows; only the trees now had fresh green leaves.

"Isn't this strange?" Anne thought to herself. "When I came here in February, everything appeared lifeless. But now, I can see life blossoming everywhere."

Fences of azaleas were blooming in the distance but were still visible from her windows. They wove a delightfully vivid green carpet that seemed to add to the welcoming beauty spring was showing Anne. The sweet song of birds filled the air, and their music relayed messages of beauty, hope, and love.

"Oh, Lord Jesus," Anne prayed within herself, "I can't thank you enough for all the love and blessings that I have received in the last few weeks. I know that you will be by my side once again in the coming weeks to help me fight off this cancer. I only ask that you give me your grace and your guiding light to help me get through these dark times. Please give me your love and blessings forever."

All of her surroundings were reminiscent of her successful initial battle with leukemia. The hospital and volunteer staff was so caring that she always felt at home. Several cards and large bouquets of flowers were already waiting for her. Those moving gestures reminded her just how many lives she had touched over the years, and it was obvious that they were keen to repay her love and kindness.

At that given moment, Anne was on the prayer list of several hundred churches in places as distinct as the US, Taiwan, Africa, India, and Europe. Shelton had been so active in Christian activities across the globe that the news of Anne's illness spread quickly across the oceans and over the continents. Over a thousand members of the Westminster Presbyterian Church where her husband preached regularly shared a website to update the world on her health status. A blogger consistently maintained a message board devoted exclusively for people to send their prayers for Anne. It was evident that Anne was reaping so many good things from what she had sown throughout her life.

Connie stayed with her that night. Although she was tired and fatigued, Anne couldn't sleep well because of the frequent interruptions of hospital staff poking and prodding her every so often to conduct various tests. She managed to close her eyes around midnight but was awakened again at 5:00 a.m. by the nursing staff so that they could check her blood pressure, temperature, and heart rate. A few hours later, the first intravenous infusions began. Anne knew exactly what to expect. The predictability of the events left Anne more comfortable than the last time. She was also much healthier this time around, with normal blood counts and no detectable leukemia cells.

After receiving the initial infusions of nausea medication and steroids, Anne saw the nurses fixing a large bag with clear liquid, unlike the blood red color of the last round of chemo. As soon as the liquid started dripping into her veins, she folded her hands and began what would seem to most to be a strange prayer. She prayed to the Lord that the liquid poisons slowly entering her would be able to spread through her entire body, reaching into all the hidden places to destroy any leukemia cells that were still lurking. She visualized the clear liquid entering her body and attacking the few hidden, angry, and deformed leukemic cells wherever they were found. She could almost feel the chemo pass through the narrow channels of her blood stream in its pursuit of the hideous cells. It was like a war was raging, with the innocent healthy tissues of her body serving as collateral damage on the battlefield. The lining of her mouth, stomach, and intestine was getting in the way of the chemotherapy, and the indiscriminate firing of the poisonous chemicals was taking its toll on them.

Anne finally fell asleep. By the time she woke up, the first of the six doses was complete. It was entirely different this time. She barely even realized that it was over. Anne didn't even have headaches or nausea, let alone seizures or vision distortions. Anne thanked the Lord for helping her through this first dosage in such a painless and comfortable manner.

The next infusions passed by uneventfully. None of the doses of cytarabine troubled her at all. All fears of brain swelling and vision loss now seemed quite unfounded. The Lord was constantly helping her sail through treatment without incident. Before she knew it, the infusions were done.

Prior to her discharge, Wendy and Dr. Spitzer came by again to discuss what would come next.

"Anne, everything has gone very well this time around. We did not have any complications! You can go home, but for the next few days, I want you to go to Dr. Patel's office for a daily injection of granulocyte colony stimulating factor. He will also check your blood count every day. As soon as your white blood count reaches 5,000 per cubic millimeter, we will get you back here and place you on a special machine that can separate and harvest stem cells from your blood."

"This is great! My prayers were answered once again. I knew that the Lord would help me through this. When do we need to get more chemo after this?" Anne asked in excitement.

"After the stem cells have been collected, we can discuss administering two more cycles of the same treatment and also plan on potential bone marrow transplantation. This is still months away, so I don't want to go into too much detail; our plans may well change. Of course, we will carry out multiple bone marrow biopsies during this time to see how you're holding up!"

Anne went home on May 2. Although she was hoping for a peaceful and relaxing time with the family, her routine was slightly altered by her daily visits to my clinic. We would check her blood count regularly and see when Dr. Spitzer thought the time was right to collect stem cells from her blood.

She had forgotten to ask the transplant coordinator in Greenville about the stem cell collection process; hence she posed her questions to me.

"Can you elaborate more on this whole stem cell collection procedure that I am supposed to be going through, Dr. Patel? Do you have any experience with it?" she asked.

"I'll be honest with you, Anne. This isn't my field of expertise. The little I know is from a few months of training on leukemia during my time in England. Please understand that I am not an expert on leukemia or transplants. At the same time, I don't think the methods have changed very much since then, so I can tell you what I do know. I can use one of my famous analogies to explain the process to you!

"The concept of a stem cell transplant is a lot like a farm. Bone marrow is basically a field. Just like a farm has fertilized soil to provide plants with everything they need to grow, bone marrow contains all the nutrients and the microenvironment necessary for your stem cells to multiply and grow. Whenever a country is lacking a particular crop, farmers will plant their fertilized soil with the seeds of that crop until it grows enough to replenish the shortage. Just like that, whenever the body is short in numbers of any type of cell, the bone marrow receives a signal to begin producing that particular cell. The stem cells will start replicating and maturing into whatever cells are needed until the shortage is resolved." I paused for a second to see if Anne understood what I was saying.

"Wow! I never imagined how complex the human body could be! Please go on. From your descriptions, it seems that only God is capable of designing a system this complex!" Anne was amazed at the complexities of the human body.

"Well, Anne, the human body is a lot more complex than you can ever imagine. But for now, let me focus on explaining what is relevant to understanding the procedure you will soon undergo. Now that all of your leukemia cells have hopefully been destroyed, we will give you doses of white blood cell boosters called granulocyte colony stimulating factor. This chemical will artificially stimulate your bone marrow to produce more stem cells that will eventually make it to your blood stream. Once your white blood cell count is over 5,000 per cubic millimeters, we will send you back to Dr. Spitzer's office. There, they will hook you up to a special machine. This machine has microspores that your blood will circulate through. These microspores will separate peripheral spores based on size and surface proteins while returning everything else back into your blood stream."

Connie stopped me at this point to ask, "But, Dr. Patel, how can this machine distinguish one group of cells from another?"

"This is another very intriguing fact about our bodies. Each cell has a unique tag. For example, the stem cells that we are interested in harvesting carry a unique identity protein called 'CD 34,' or 'cluster differentiation antigen 34.' Only the stem cells capable of self-renewal and maturation carry this tag. Scientists have developed an antibody that can reversibly bind to this protein. Microcomputers within the cell sorter machine can then separate these cells suspended in a small amount of plasma and allow the rest of the blood to be infused back in the body."

"How will they collect the cells? Will they insert some tubes into Mom's veins?" Connie asked curiously.

"Something similar. Your mom already has a Hickman catheter, that double lumen tube they insert in the neck vein. At the time of stem cell collection, they will connect one tube so that blood comes out of her body and passes through the Cell Sorter and Separator machine. Once inside, the blood is collected in a small centrifuge that will rotate rapidly. This will churn up all the blood cells and separate them based on size. There are multiple pores for collection of the cells that we are interested in. These sieve-like openings allow stem cells to leak out into small bags along with bits of plasma. The rest of the plasma and all remaining cells are infused back through the other tube in the Hickman catheter, back into her body."

"Will this procedure be painful? Is she going to have any other symptoms? I just want to know what to expect," Connie asked.

"No, I don't believe that she will have any pain. However, during the procedure they will have to give her anticoagulants to keep her blood flowing through the machine. This may cause her calcium level to drop and could cause circumoal anesthesia, a slight tingling and numbness around her mouth and lips. I do not believe any other major side effects will occur," I replied, trying my best to alleviate her concerns.

"How will they know when they have enough stem cells?" Connie then asked.

"We can actually count the number of stem cells in each bag by checking flow cytometry. It's a technique we use to identify the percentage of cells in each bag. Once that estimate is available, we will be able to tell when we have enough cells," I replied.

"Wow, it's unbelievable how far technology has come, Dr. Patel. Thank God we have so many options available for treating cancer nowadays. But I have one last question before Mom's blood check. Is it possible that leukemia cells will contaminate her stem cells?"

Connie's last question was a very difficult one to answer.

"That's a question that may not be something we should think about at this stage," I said, trying to evade the question. But the look on Anne and Connie's face when I avoided answering was extremely painful, so I decided to continue.

"There is a possibility, very small but still real, that the leukemia cells will have contaminated her stem cells. As I explained, leukemia arises as a result of competition between normal blood precursor cells. Leukemia cells begin as normal cells. Somewhere in their life span they mutate, taking over the entire bone marrow cavity and blood stream at the expense of normal blood cells. They consume all the nutrients and push normal maturing cells to almost extinction. Leukemia cells are essentially immortal. They infiltrate tissues like the bone marrow, liver, spleen, and lymph nodes; on rare occasions they even get in the skin and brain. They invade any part of the body and multiply there, starving and killing the normal surrounding tissue that can no longer compete for nutrients. Like terrorist sleeper cells, they plant themselves unseen in the smallest places only to eventually emerge and destroy the host tissues whenever the time is ripe. They have the ability to hibernate in remote sites that are not very accessible to chemotherapy, and it is from this hibernation that relapses occur. So, to answer your question, in all honesty there is definitely a small chance of a hidden leukemia cell hibernating somewhere in such a small quantity that it can't be detected. We call this occurrence MRD, minimal residual disease. I was reluctant to discuss it with you because there is nothing that we can do to detect or avoid MRD, and I didn't want to burden you with something there is no way to fix. Only time will tell."

I saw the downtrodden look on their faces and quickly added, "Please, bear in mind that this is a rare occurrence. Most patients don't experience MRD." I wanted to be sure that I ended on a positive note.

Anne took her shot and went home. For the next seven days she received shots, but her blood count still hadn't recovered well enough. Finally, on the eighth day, her blood count made it to the threshold of 5,000 per cubic millimeter.

She was then taken back to Greenville and hooked up to the blood sorter machine. After two sessions, they collected enough stem cells for the transplantation procedure.

Summer was just round the corner. Months had gone by since Anne was diagnosed with leukemia. Her initial struggle had come to a tranquil end, with all detectable leukemia cells destroyed. Her treatments were now focused on eliminating any hidden cells that had escaped the first rounds. Visits to my office and to St. Francis Hospital for chemotherapy had become a routine occurrence for her. The next two rounds of chemotherapy were uneventful, and she didn't have any serious complications or excessive apprehension from them. Finally, the time for a bone marrow transplant arrived.

# CHAPTER 6

# THE FINAL BLOW

*If we had no winter,*
*the spring would not be so pleasant:*
*if we did not sometimes taste of adversity,*
*prosperity would not be so welcome.*
—ANNE BRADSTREET

SUMMER HAD ARRIVED. FOR ANNE, the countdown to the day of her transplant felt as tense as the countdown for the launching of an Apollo rocket–T-minus ten days and counting, T-minus nine days and counting, T-minus eight days and counting. Anne would have to be in the hospital for as long as it took for her bone marrow to recover. It could potentially take weeks or even months, depending on the quality of the stem cells that were collected from her body.

In preparation for the stem cell transplant, Anne had all of her vital organs checked: her liver, her lungs, her heart, her kidneys, and her immune system. The first half of June was spent having a different part of her body checked each day. She was also given fresh doses of vaccinations against most common illnesses. Her immune system was going to be destroyed by the procedure; they had to make sure she was as protected from disease as possible. The bone marrow transplantation was scheduled for June 22. Anne came to my office a week before.

"My oh my, Dr. Patel, we sure have come a long way. I'm going back to St. Francis next week. I don't know how long I'll be there. But I wanted to thank you for everything that you have done for me. If you don't mind, I was hoping you could explain what I should expect so I can be mentally prepared." Despite the looming procedure, Anne didn't seem to have lost any of her tranquility.

"I'm sure Dr. Spitzer's team will discuss all aspects of the procedure with you. I can tell you a little bit based on my past experience. They'll probably run you through all sorts of tests before the actual procedure. The procedure is very harsh and complex; we have to be sure your body can handle it physically. Leukemia cells often hide in bone marrow: the purpose of this procedure is to destroy the entire stem cell pool that is currently there. As collateral damage, many regular cells that divide rapidly will also be killed," I explained.

"How will it affect me? How will I feel? Will I get sick?" Anne then asked.

"I'm afraid that this procedure is worse than any of the ones you've undergone so far. Your mouth will get sore to the point that you will not be able to eat or drink without pain for a few days after the procedure. Your blood count will drop to the point that you will need multiple transfusions to keep your red blood cell and platelet count at a minimum level. Your immune system is going to be destroyed. While you will be given antibiotics to prevent any secondary opportunistic diseases, you will still be vulnerable to many different kinds of infection. Bacterial infections are the most common nuisance, but it's the fungal or yeast infections in your liver or lungs that can pose life-threatening complications. At the same time, I know that your treatments have all been relatively smooth before, and with faith, perseverance, and the will of the Lord, I think that you will sail through even this transplant. I just want to make sure that you are aware that this procedure is more taxing than any that you have had to endure so far. Oh, don't be alarmed if you smell an odor of fish when they begin infusing the stem cells. It's from a compound called DMSO that they use to preserve the stem cells in a subzero temperature," I concluded.

"I know this sounds silly, but I want to ask you something else. After the existing bone marrow is destroyed, will they just … inject the harvested stem cells back inside my bone marrow?" Anne asked curiously.

"No, they won't. The harvested cells will be infused into your blood stream," I replied.

"How will they start regenerating inside the bone marrow then? Isn't that where they should be?"

"Think of stem cells like you would birds. In winter, birds fly south to Florida for shelter but come back to Alaska in the summer. If you release any bird into Alaska during a summer, it will still fly to Florida eventually. Similarly, stem cells will eventually make their own way into the bone marrow," I answered.

"You sound quite poetic. Could you please explain exactly how they'll return to my bone marrow?" Anne asked.

"The stem cells have a distinct homing phenomenon. They are empowered with certain signaling pathways that can sense their tissue microenvironment. When the presence of bone marrow is detected, they will enter cavities in the marrow called sinusoids. These sinusoids are multiple small channels with narrow passages filled with blood. When infused stem cells pass through bone marrow sinusoids, they are trapped in the marrow. Cell signals determine the local micro chemical compounds, and they will settle in the appropriate places. Once settled, they begin a process called self renewal, in which single stem cells will produce multiple copies of themselves. Once a sufficient number of cells are produced, one pool will end the process and will remain ready to start replicating again if need be. The other pool will slowly start maturing into different categories of blood cells like neutrophils, lymphocytes, red blood cells, and platelets. The process excites me a lot, and it's the only regret I have in not pursuing a career in a teaching hospital."

Anne was awestruck at the intricacy of the process. "The power of the Lord's creation is fascinating! Only God could have made such a complex process. Please go on, Dr. Patel. I am enjoying this conversation much more than I thought I would."

"Its funny you share the same trust in God and nature as I do. The human body has always been such a fascinating and complex machine. Man has never produced anything even close to that complex, and scientists still aren't clear on how some mechanisms the body uses actually work. There have always been many controversies between evolution and the biblical beliefs of creation. I can tell you that even though I am a man of science with many research publications to my credit, the deeper I dig into the mysteries of life and the human body, the more convinced I am that there is at least some part played by a higher power. There is so much order and discipline from the microscopic to the macroscopic level that evolution alone cannot explain it. Everything from cellular respiration to intracellular signaling pathways and intercellular cell adhesion molecules facilitating communication between cells is far too complex to have developed on its own. That is like saying a series of nuts, bolts, and bits of metal fell off a shelf and through sheer luck happened to fall in such a way that they created a working internal combustion engine on the floor. It is just far too complex to be explained by mere chance. You have to believe that someone is watching over all of this. It is impossible otherwise. The more research I did, the closer I came to this conclusion. Have you ever heard of the concepts of microcosm and macrocosm?" I said.

"The terms ring a bell, but I don't really remember from where. Can you explain them?" Anne replied.

"Whatever physical as well as biological phenomenon we see in the outwardly visible universe and world is happening in a predictive and repetitive cycle. Everything has a predictable order to it. Whether it is a microcosm of electrons orbiting a nucleus in an atom or a macrocosm that spans an entire galaxy—all will have a cycle. To give you an example, look at the cycle of plant life. As a small plant grows and matures, it bears flowers and fruits. Little birds eat the fruits and fly away. As they fly away, they drop the seeds of the fruits on the ground in locations away from the original plant. These droppings will then bring in new plants from the same species. The cycle of plant bearing fruit will continue. Other plants do the same with butterflies and bumblebees carrying their pollen for them. The reproductive cycles within flower-bearing plants sustain the existence of plants, insects, and birds. Everything has such cycles, and in these cycles is the beauty of creation. Even stars and galaxies have their own cycles."

I took a breath before continuing. "In your case, there is another cyclic process that will be at work on a scale placing it in a microcosm. The stem cells that have been harvested and collected will enter your blood circulation where cell signaling pathways will direct them to the locations in the bone marrow where they will mature."

"You mean the cells talk to each other?" Anne said.

"Yes, they communicate with each other by producing and releasing certain chemicals that serve as signals. They are also capable of recognizing each other and sometimes even destroying each other. Coming back to your case, stem cells will find their way to the bone marrow sinusoids with the help of other cells that direct them. Within the bone marrow, cell adhesion molecules will help them cling in the bone marrow. Surrounding cells, including fibroblasts which ensure appropriate nutrient balance in the cells similar to nitrogen-producing bacteria in the soil, and other cells will start producing chemicals called cytokines that help stem cells kick-start their life cycle again. Isn't it just amazing?" I said.

"It is indeed. This really is wonderful information. It's almost too difficult for me to understand, but it's still too amazing to ignore," Anne responded in awe of the mysteries surrounding life.

"This is just in the realm of the human body, where I am familiar with the complex processes involved. However, there is even more convincing evidence in the field of physics. In the microcosm, subatomic particles are suspended in spaces so tiny even the most powerful microscopes can't see them. That same force allows electrons, protons, and neutrons to coexist in an atom without reacting. You see this even in astrophysics. The same force keeps the moon in the Earth's orbit, the Earth in sun's orbit, and the solar system in the Milky Way. To see the power of these forces, look at what happens when they are interrupted. The only time science has managed to do this is in a very crude manner with the atomic bomb. And despite the crude nature of this device, you can see how much power it contains.

"What I believe is that these forces keep the world in order and that they are part of a grand scheme of divine origins. When we open our eyes, we see the same life forces percolating all around us. We just need to be open-minded. For me, being a scientist and working with stem cell expansion has helped enhance my understanding of divinity," I concluded. At that point I stopped and politely summed up the discussion by explaining some other ins and outs of the bone marrow transplant.

Anne came to me seeking information on bone marrow transplants and went home with a better understanding of how spirituality and religion could be intertwined. She also went home ready to tackle the upcoming transplant with the ultimate punch.

The days flew by, and "day zero" finally arrived. She went back to St. Francis and was given the same room as before. She was surrounded by the same staff and by the same positive aura.

A new identity badge was applied to her wrist downstairs. Many bouquets of flowers were awaiting her in the room. Once again, she was dressed in a hospital gown. And as usual, Dr. Spitzer arrived late that evening, as strangely dressed as ever, with Wendy by his side.

In his booming voice, he began by saying, "Hello, young lady! Are you ready for the season finale of our battle against leukemia? I know you aren't a fan of soaps. But hopefully this will be your last appearance at St. Francis Hospital! As a patient at least, that is. It's not that I don't like seeing you, but I think you've been my patient for quite long enough now, and it's our hope that the next time we see each other, it won't be as doctor and patient but rather as friends!"

"Thank you, Dr. Spitzer! I'm ready! Dr. Patel has prepared me pretty thoroughly for this last home run. I pretty much know what to expect. But I want to hear your take on what will happen now," Anne said.

Dr. Spitzer replied, "Today is day minus-five. In exactly five days, we will infuse your bone marrow back into your body. Between now and then, we will condition your body for reception of the stem cells that we collected earlier. Our aim is to destroy your hematopoietic system completely so that no traces of cancerous cells are left behind. Once again we will place the double tubes into your neck veins. We will carry out several tests on your blood and urine along with chest x-rays and an electrocardiogram to ensure that your body is still capable of handling the physical stress and side effects of the procedure."

"Are you going to use the same chemicals that you used before?" Anne asked. Better the devil you know than the devil you don't.

"No, Anne, the chemo combination this time is called BUCY. It stands for busulphan and Cytoxan. These two chemotherapy agents have been in existence for several decades. Together, in large enough doses, they are capable of wiping your bone marrow of all stem cells. Once we achieve this, we will infuse the stem cells we harvested several months ago to allow the bone marrow to rebuild itself. We will check your bone marrow for successful grafting every other week. I'm hoping that we will see some positive activities within the month," Dr. Spitzer replied.

"Dr. Patel has already explained those aspects of recovery and side effects. I pretty much know what to expect. I'm ready, so let's get on with the show!" Anne said eagerly.

The official countdown was reflected in Anne's chart and on all papers pertaining to her stay in the hospital. The evening of day minus-five was quite busy. She went back and forth to different departments for various tests. Phlebotomists came by to draw large amounts of blood. The next morning brought with it day minus-four. She was connected to an intravenous infusion, first with saline, then with steroids and anti-nausea medication. She had to swallow twenty-five pills, some of them oral chemotherapy drugs and others antibiotics and antiviral medication given as precautionary measures. Finally, a massive dose of the anti-neoplastic agent Cytoxan was administered. The dose was so large that she was connected to an indwelling catheter to flush out any excess medications in her urinary bladder.

Day minus-three, day minus-two, and day minus-one passed by in similar fashion. The impact of chemotherapy was becoming more and more obvious. What began simply as sore mouth became more painful by the minute, until any hot or spicy food was intolerable. Soon after, she developed oral ulcers, which called for even more medications. Her blood count was also dropping at the same time.

Finally day zero came. It was June 22, the day after the first official day of summer. Carolyn, one of Gary Spitzer's nurses specializing in infusion of marrow products, came in with what looked like a bag of frozen strawberry sorbet. In the bag were the frozen stem cells that would soon be infused back into Anne. Carolyn placed the bag in lukewarm liquid so that it would thaw. Within a half hour, the thawing was complete. The pink colored liquid was what all Anne's hopes now rested upon. If it did its job, she could have her normal life back.

Carolyn brought the bag to Anne's bedside and hooked it into a pole. She gave Anne a dose of steroids and Benadryl to prevent any potential allergic reactions, which was ironic since the cells had once been part of Anne's body. After that, she connected the bag to a catheter in her large vein.

Once the bag of stem cells was attached to the cannula, Anne could see the liquid slowly filtering into her vein lines. She could see each drop of the life-prolonging liquid drip through the tubing, one drop of life at a time.

Anne closed her eyes and started praying. "Oh Lord, please bless each and every drop of this liquid containing my stem cells so that any possible leukemia cells left behind will be destroyed. May these stem cells bring my marrow back to normal. I know that you will do what is best for both of us, my Lord Jesus. Please, Jesus, listen to my prayers and be with me on this journey." She fell asleep with this prayer on her lips and dreamt that she had been cured of leukemia.

"Anne." A gentle voice broke through her sleep. It was Shelton. She slowly came back to a waking state. She heard his gentle voice saying, "It's over, Anne. Your stem cells are all infused. Dr. Spitzer did what he had to. Now it is up to the Lord. Let us pray that your stem cells quickly find their home inside your bone marrow and start regenerating with amazing speed. I can't wait to have you healthy and home again."

"I know, Shelton ... I can't wait either," Anne feebly replied. The ulcers from the chemo made any speech extremely painful; she had severe mucositis, a destruction of the fine lining of all the cells coating the inside of her mouth.

She drew a harsh breath and whispered, "I can't wait for this to be over."

The pain was so excruciating that the nurse gave her morphine. She fell asleep soon after. Dr. Spitzer also gave her a bottle of liquid Lidocaine--a local anesthetic to help control the pain.

The next week proved to be the worst one she had ever had in her life. Her mouth was completely raw with ulcers. The difficulty in swallowing food caused her to lose three pounds. Even swallowing her medicine was painful. Her throat was constantly parched, but bearing that was less painful than the agony that drinking water put her through. She lost more weight. Yet behind the agony of pain, her faint smile still lingered. Despite the agony she suffered, she still did not lose her composure. Within a week, she began the recovery process.

In the days that followed that week of hell, her body recovered with leaps and bounds. As if the Lord himself had touched it, her body started healing inch by inch on an hour-by-hour basis. Her recovery was associated with a surge in her white blood cells, particularly the neutrophils. Finally, the infused stem cells settled in the bone marrow and found the nutrients necessary for their growth. Her own microcosm was becoming a haven of law and order once again.

Infused stem cells settling down in her marrow gave rise to multitudes of different lineages of blood cells, each in turn maturing to take on new functions. She could feel the healing power of the neutrophils, moving in with necessary cytokines to repair the ulcers and gaps created in her mouth by the damage from chemotherapy. Her pain was pretty much gone, her ulcers healed, and she was able to eat and drink once again, with her blood count recovery at the heart of her resurgence.

It seemed clear to her that the human body was a unique living microcosm that was far beyond a simple biological phenomenon and had a power of recovery that was unfathomable.

Anne's recovery was exponential. She continued to improve daily. She had become extremely weak. Even though her mouth, blood count, and weight were all improving, she had been in bed for almost a fortnight. Standing up and walking even a few yards was now exhausting for her. It was de-conditioning, an illness that usually appeared after prolonged hospitalization. Her muscles had atrophied from lack of use over an extended period of time. Although it wasn't very serious, she would have to fight through her exhaustion and lack of strength to use her muscles in order to recover their former vigor.

Wendy came in to give her another bone marrow test. This was the most crucial moment of her life that she was aware of so far. Dr. Spitzer came in person to discuss the results with her and her husband.

"Hello, sweet lady! I have extremely good news! Your stem cells have engrafted well in the bone marrow. Your blood count is also recovered. While most potential side effects have waned, you have developed jaundice. In addition, I think that you have developed a condition called hepatic veno-occlusive disorder, a well-recognized but not well-understood complication."

"You are confusing me, Dr. Spitzer. How is this good news? How is it that you say I have recovered but I still suffer from a complication? What happens now?" Anne asked, extremely confused.

"Well, I have been keeping a close watch on all the numbers, and it seems the jaundice won't affect you much. The veno-occlusive disease in the liver is recovering. I don't think the jaundice will cause any residual issues. You just need to take a pill to prevent it from worsening," Dr. Spitzer said reassuringly.

"Good. Does that mean I can go home soon?" Anne asked eagerly.

"Certainly, as soon as you feel up to it. I don't think you will face many risks of infection or bleeding. Your blood count will normalize in due time. Hopefully, I won't ever have to see you as a patient again!" he told her.

"Can we open a bottle of champagne?" Shelton asked.

"No, celebration is still very premature. Not yet. Not for another five years," Dr. Spitzer said. He sounded very serious.

"Why did he have to say that?" Anne was asking herself. "Couldn't he have waited for a few weeks before reminding me that leukemia could slip back at any time?"

She managed to erase his pessimistic words on the drive home.

# CHAPTER 7

# VICTORY IS OURS

*Learn to get in touch with the silence within yourself, and know that everything in this life has purpose.*
*There are no mistakes, no coincidences.*
*All events are blessings given to us to learn from.*
—ELISABETH KÜBLER-ROSS

ANNE'S INTENSE STRUGGLE AGAINST LEUKEMIA was finally coming to a lull. No more injections, no more chemo, no more hospital beds, and above all, no more anxieties about dying. The Lord Jesus had saved her, and she was very thankful to Him. The thousands of prayers people around the world had spoken on her behalf had certainly been heard. With the Lord on her side, she had emerged from the path of suffering and pain unharmed.

She went home the first week of July. The family was in a celebratory mood despite Dr. Spitzer's warnings. In her modest Rock Hill home, bouquets of fragrant flowers accompanied by hundreds of letters and cards filled every corner. As weak and feeble as Anne was, her spirit at finally being in control of her life again was unmatchable. The physical limitations from de-conditioning were easily overcome, and her eternal smile masked the amount of trauma and suffering she had been through in the past months. Her entire family, including her grandmother

Lucille, her daughters, her grandchildren, and her dog, was at the door awaiting her homecoming.

Despite the familiarity of everything, Anne felt a bit odd and different during this homecoming—not because of her weakness. Despite emerging victoriously, leukemia had changed her life forever. She wanted to let God decide the course of her future actions rather than proceeding ahead with her own desires and selfish interests. Witnessing the Lord's blessings and guidance during her periods of suffering and pain had changed her outlook on life. From now on, life was going to be lived differently. No matter what came her way, she was only going to carry out ordained actions inspired by the Lord. She was not going to devote even an ounce of worry to the possibility of leukemia coming back. She knew that as a human being, she had no control over that. Therefore, she resolved not worry about something that she couldn't control.

She underwent intensive physical therapy to overcome her deconditioning. She spent two to three hours a day doing exercises and found that her recovery was a lot faster than expected. Like Dr. Spitzer predicted, her blood count started rising soon.

On August 2, about a month after she came home, Anne came to my office for follow-up blood work. Shelton and Connie came with her. Physical therapy was over by now, and she had recovered completely.  She came in feeling particularly healthy and upbeat. "I feel great, Dr. Patel! I know that my blood count is going to be normal today. I can feel that I am healed already."

"That's great, Anne! Let's see if the machine agrees with what are you thinking. I will be quite happy as well if that is the case. I have one question for you, though. When most patients come in my door, they are nervous and melancholic. What is it that gives you this sort of attitude?" I asked.

"I'm not sure, Dr. Patel, but for some reason I just feel blessed today. I can do anything I want without being tired. I have no physical symptoms; it just seems like today will be a good day!"

"She's right, Dr. Patel! All of her blood counts are normal!" April said with a big smile when she walked in with a copy of Anne's blood work.

"Didn't I tell you, Dr. Patel? I've learned to listen to my body!" Anne happily responded, confident in her instinct.

"I see that, Anne! Well now, you are officially in remission! Time to celebrate!" I was ecstatic to see that her blood count had recovered completely and that her last bone marrow test showed no evidence of residual disease.

"Are you sure this is the time to celebrate? Does this mean that I am cured of leukemia?" Anne asked, praying that she could forget about leukemia once and for all.

"Well, what I can say is that you are in remission. If you stay in remission for three to four years, then I can say you are cured. For all practical purposes, time is what we need to ask of God. As each month passes, the risk of leukemia coming back grows less and less. Being an eternal optimist, I would like to think that your leukemia will never come back and I only have to see you as a friend and not as a patient in the future." Despite the difference in outlook, I shared Dr. Spitzer's deep concern for the well being of my patients.

"I like the way you put it, Kashyap!" Shelton said. "Dr. Spitzer sometimes sounds less optimistic." They distinctly recalled Dr. Spitzer's warning of not celebrating for five years.

"Well, Shelton, Gary and I make a good pair. It's a case of good cop/bad cop. We are both on opposite ends of the prognosis spectrum, but at times it's good for you to get opinions from both sides. He's right; to be sure, we have to wait five years. While the risk of recurrence in years four and five is almost zero, it still is not quite zero. There have been rare cases when recurrence occurred even in late year five. And also, Gary has a lot more experience in leukemia than I do. Bear in mind that I don't even have the facilities necessary to treat leukemia in my office. When it comes to leukemia, he is a better judge of outcome. But at the same time, I think that living a life of anxiety is counter-productive. If the leukemia does come back in any of my patients, I encourage each one to live every day God has given them to the fullest. If you spend every day worrying, you will ruin whatever time you have left. Live each day with the mindset that you are cured and can do anything you want; don't worry about future relapses. We have done everything we can; it is all in the Lord's hands now. We can only take each day, week, month, and year as it comes. We can't predict the future. For all that we know, you may be cured of leukemia but die in a car accident on the way home. We don't know what is coming next. All we can do now is trust that God will take care of us no matter what," I said, trying to explain the difference between Gary's approach and mine.

"Well then, what is next? Where do we go now?" Shelton asked. He was hoping that he could plan that long-awaited trip to Taiwan with Anne now that she was in remission.

"I think that we should have a bone marrow test next week. After that, we will have one more three months later. Even if both of these marrow specimens reveal that she is still in remission, I want take another blood check and bone marrow test every three months. But I still want to see her on a monthly basis," I explained, giving them the rough schedule for the next year before adding, "I don't think we should make a schedule beyond that quite yet."

"We can't thank you enough for everything that you have done for us, Dr. Patel," Connie began tearfully. "You are like a godsend for us. If there is anything that we can do for you now or in the future, please don't hesitate to ask."

Anne came in the following week for her bone marrow test. As predicted, her marrow was clean. There were no detectable leukemia cells left behind. If the tests in the next few years were all similar, she would be cured. Another leukemia patient of mine once told me that he wished he could be put into a state of sleep for five years so that he could wake up cured. That was the opposite of what Anne wanted. She knew that whatever happened from then on would be God's will. He had already answered her prayers during the leukemia treatment, and she knew that he had her best interests at heart. She couldn't ask more of him. She decided that she would take my advice; from then on, she wanted to live every second of her life to the fullest degree, serving her Lord and her fellow human beings to the maximum possible extent.

Her life was pretty well back to normal. Leukemia made its exit from her life the same day it made its exit out of her marrow. Her monthly blood work results came back as normal for the next three months. Each day after her transplantation was counted as an additional victory.

But on the hundredth day after her transplant, something felt different. Anne woke up with severe pains shooting down both her legs. It was so painful that she could barely move. She also felt like she had been hit with the flu. It was eerily similar to what she experienced at the beginning of the year, when the cancer had first been diagnosed. Her mind immediately jumped to various possibilities. Surely the leukemia hadn't returned?

No, it can't be, Anne decided. She had bone marrow and blood tests just a month ago, and both were negative for leukemic cells. She kept her thoughts to herself, thinking that the pain would pass, but if anything, the pain intensified. When late afternoon fell, she called Connie at work.

"Connie, the sides of both of my legs are hurting. I can barely move them. What do you think is happening? Should we go to see Dr. Patel?"

"I'll be right home, Mom. Just sit tight for a few minutes," Connie replied, her voice full of panic. She rushed home immediately and along the way called my office to ask if I was available to see Anne as soon as possible. One of my assistants told her I was free near the end of the day, and Connie had an appointment booked for her mother.

When she arrived home, Connie immediately examined her mom's legs, looking in particular for red spots indicative of leukemia resurgence. There were none, and Connie breathed a sigh of relief. At least Anne's platelets were normal, and that lessened the chance of leukemia being back with a vengeance. But their minds were still not completely at ease when they walked through my door later that day.

"Hi, Anne! Hello, Connie!" I greeted them. "What brings you here today? I didn't think I'd see you for at least another month. Weren't you just here two weeks ago?"

"My legs are hurting, Dr. Patel. This is exactly how the leukemia began last time. I'm sure that it must be nothing, but I need you to tell me that it really is nothing! "Anne said. She was being very cautious this time around.

"Well, since your blood was clear in the last test, I don't think we should be overly concerned, but it's always better to be safe than sorry. Let me take a look at you, and then we can carry out another blood count and anything else that will tell us what we are dealing with," I replied.

I examined her thoroughly. There weren't any obvious signs to be worried about. There were no oral ulcers or bleeding spots. Her hips were a bit more tender than they normally should be, but that could have been due to the speed of her bone marrow division. If it was faster than usual, it could have led to the leg pains. Her tests came back fine. Her blood count was even better than it was on her last visit. All blood cell lines were normal.

I reassured her that nothing seemed to be amiss and that the leg pains were probably due to over-production of bone marrow stem cells, or perhaps from overexertion on Anne's behalf. Now that she had resumed all the activities of her regular life, some muscle fatigue was to be reasonably expected. Neither was anything to worry about.

Although I couldn't see anything unusual in Anne's pain, she could. Maybe she was instinctively aware of something that all my tests had missed. Anne had picked up the skill of listening to her own body, and it was telling her that all was not well.

What I could detect was that Anne herself seemed different, but I couldn't quite figure out how. It wasn't her attitude: she was definitely not depressed or overly concerned. All she wanted to do was affirm what she thought was happening in her body.

No matter how much I reassured her, I could tell that she took the leg pains much more seriously than I did. I couldn't quite detect what was different about the way she reacted to my news that there truly was nothing to worry about. Those thoughts faded when I then went in to see another patient, and I soon forgot about the indescribable feeling that Anne was exuding.

## CHAPTER 8

# THE BEGINNING OF THE END OR THE END OF THE BEGINNING

*God, grant me the serenity to accept the things I cannot change,*
*Courage to change the things I can,*
*And the wisdom to know the difference.*
—Reinhold Niebuhr

ANNE CAME IN FOR HER regular follow-up appointment, accompanied by Shelton and Connie, on October 25, exactly three weeks after her episode with the leg pains. It was now day 121 after her bone marrow transplant. Fall had just arrived, bringing the first cold air of the season with it. My parking lot was full of newly dropped yellow leaves. The sun was now hidden behind a cloudy and overcast sky. The air held a very premature chill along with an unusual gloom. Anne was the last patient scheduled for the day, and it was almost five in the afternoon when I went in to examine her.

As far as physical appearances were concerned, Anne looked good. Her skin still retained an excellent color, and her face was lit as always with that bright smile everyone she came into contact with had come to love. And yet, there was something about her face that was slightly discomforting to me. It appeared hollow, almost as if she was blissfully ignorant of her surroundings. This, however, was a face I could interpret. It was the face of someone to whom little mattered.

By now her leg pains and the flu-like symptoms had disappeared entirely. As usual, I was smiling and jovial during our conversation. I asked whether she was feeling anything unusual, and she denied any abnormal symptoms after the leg pains disappeared. I examined her thoroughly and, once again, didn't find any abnormalities whatsoever.

I then remarked, "Another month gone by, and still you seem fine! Let me just take a look at the blood work results, and then you can go home. Our next meeting will be in 2006!"

It was the last week of October, and this was going to be Anne's last visit to my office for the year. With each passing month, the chances of recurrence were lessening, and it seemed like the clouds ahead were slowly disappearing.

Still, Anne was quiet. "It's no problem, Dr. Patel. We can wait for the blood count results," she replied faintly. She was much more reticent today than during any of her previous visits. Was there something she was concerned about? I made up my mind to ask her after we had reviewed her blood work.

There was a knock on the door. April was waiting outside.

"Come in, April!" I said, wondering why she was standing in the doorway.

"Um, Dr. Patel? Could I talk to you outside for a minute?"

I told Anne I'd be back in a minute.

I walked outside and asked April what the problem was. Wordlessly, she handed over the results of Anne's blood work.

I glanced at it for less than a second before realizing that something was very wrong. Denial was my first response.

"Are you sure you had a good sample? Are you sure the specimen wasn't overly diluted? Blood must have been caught up and slowed down in the tube! Maybe blood clotted either inside the butterfly or inside the EDTA tube."

I could think of a million different reasons for what I saw in front of me except for the most obvious and most painful. April merely responded by shaking her head at all of my queries. I decided to look at the blood film myself. Perhaps her sample was mislabeled. But that wasn't the case; hers was the only blood sample drawn in the last half hour. That meant that the blood results could only have come from one thing.

Walking back into that room was very difficult. No amount of experience ever prepares doctors well enough for difficult, life-altering conversations that follow blood tests that announce cancer. I came in with my head hanging low from disappointment. It felt even harder to form the words because I had reassured her just a few minutes ago that nothing was wrong. Had I been too optimistic? Did I need to change the way I thought about cancer? I couldn't think of the answers to these questions at the moment.

I began cautiously. "Anne, your blood count is not totally normal. Your white blood cell count has dropped somewhat, and so have your platelets. Although there isn't an overly pronounced drop, it is still significant, and this worries me." There wasn't more that I could say at that point.

Connie immediately understood the words I had left unstated. "Is her leukemia back? Could it be a lab error? Are you sure this was her sample? Could there be another reason besides leukemia for this abnormality?"

Connie was visibly upset. Her initial reaction was just like mine, and like April did for me, I slowly shook my head at each of her queries.

I glanced at Shelton. His face had completely fallen, and he seemed to have suddenly entered a state of severe melancholy. He couldn't even express himself, and so he let Connie voice his concerns.

I shook my head and said, "I have looked into all of these possibilities, but I'm afraid the results are accurate. I have no doubt that this is her blood count. But, we do have some hope. There still could be an external cause for this, aside from leukemia relapse," I said. This was true; while my first reaction was to think the leukemia had returned, upon reflection there were other possible, less severe causes for the drop.

"Really? Can it be reversed?" Connie asked.

"It depends on what caused the drop. If it's a depletion of the stem cell pool, it could have occurred for a variety of reasons, and we can recover her blood count. Some medications sometimes lower blood count." My thinking was wistful, but it was certainly possible. I was still against blaming leukemia until all other possibilities were exhausted.

"Thank God!" Connie expressed. "What next?"

"After a week we can take another blood test. Maybe her counts will have improved by then. At the moment, I think that we should have a bone marrow test tomorrow as well. In my opinion, that will indicate what is actually going on in Anne's body and tell us what direction to take. I'll have the staff work you into my schedule. What do you think, Anne? You have been quiet so far," I said.

Desperate to prevent overly-negative thinking, I added, "There is still hope that this is something other than a leukemia relapse."

"I'm not worried, Dr. Patel. Every word you said made sense. Since I awoke with leg pains a few weeks ago, I am more acutely aware of God's presence in my life. When I wake up, I look outside at the beautiful sky with its white fluffy clouds, and I am aware of the immensity of his presence in all of creation. Hearing the birds sing, looking at the beautiful flowers, and hearing the gentle wind blowing between trees reminds me that all nature proclaims God's power and presence. Why should I be worried? If he decides to call me to my heavenly home, I am not afraid. Jesus promised that he had prepared a place for me and that he would come again and receive me unto himself, that where he is, there I may be also."

It wasn't despair that I was seeing in Anne. It was the most graceful acceptance of any ending to the story of a human that I had ever seen. I could see God in one place that Anne hadn't mentioned. He was present in her grace, poise, and trust that whatever happened, she would be well taken care of by him. I was in such a state of wonder at Anne's grace that I couldn't really respond.

It turned out that my schedule was absolutely packed, and I couldn't see her until the next Monday for the bone marrow test. The next forty-eight hours were difficult even for me to pass. In my field, you have to be open to the possibility that half of your patients will die, no matter how hard you fight for them. If you weren't open to that possibility, you would break down in your first year of practice. But for even the most hardened oncologist, every once in a while a patient comes along and deeply touches the heart with everything about him or her. Anne was one of those patients, and I was genuinely afraid for her.

She duly came in for the test, as calm and as composed as ever. She went home while the results were processed. I decided to get the results myself. I looked down and began to read them. What stared back up at me was harsh truth. With a heavy heart, I asked Anne to come back into the office the next morning.

She came in with Connie and Shelton. I purposely kept them at the end of the morning schedule so that I could have all the time I needed with them. Lunch could wait. Before they came in, I called Gary Spitzer and told him about Anne's abnormal bone marrow. He was extremely saddened by it as well: he knew explicitly what it meant.

The Sanford family could sense by the look on my face that my wishful thinking had been for naught.

"Anne, I'm afraid that your condition has indeed relapsed. It isn't full blown leukemia, rather it is a stage called myelodysplasia, or refractory anemia with excess blasts. In common language, it is known as preleukemia. I'm sorry … I wish I could have had better news for you."

Connie was visibly shaking as she asked, "Now what?"

Shelton was trying to hold back his emotions while holding Anne's right hand between his own two hands.

"I spoke with Gary Spitzer and worked out a plan we think will be best. We both believe and agree that the best thing to do is to start treating her with a compound called Vidaza, or 5-azacytidine. It is a form of treatment that helps immature cells achieve maturation and thus can potentially reverse the myelodysplasia before it becomes leukemia," I replied in a very low and dispassionate tone. I was looking for words to reassure and comfort them. But there weren't many, and I didn't want to conceal my uncertainty in the path they would soon be taking.

"Can we really reverse the process? How often have you seen this happening? How long does this medication take to work? Do we have to go to Greenville? Can we do it here?" Connie asked in rapid succession, her body still trembling from the shock of hearing the word "relapse" come out of my mouth.

"I'll be honest, Connie, I really don't know. I don't know how long it will take for it to work. The only times I have studied its effectiveness have been when people are diagnosed with myelodysplasia in the first juncture, not for people like Anne who are diagnosed with full-blown leukemia. In those cases it has sometimes reversed the myelodysplasia and prevented it from becoming leukemia. But there haven't been studies on its effectiveness in the situation we are facing, and it has seldom been used post-relapse. These are uncharted waters; even I don't know what to expect. That is why I am not sure if the possibility of reversing this process is realistic. We can certainly do it here. At the same time, Gary is searching for bone marrow matches for her. Please understand that Vidaza is only a temporary measure. Even if she responds as we hope she will, it will only be transitory. If we want to prolong life for a significant amount of time, we have to undergo a MUD transplant from a donor."

Connie and Shelton both burst into tears. I was holding some back myself. I could understand their emotions. It was obvious that all these actions were merely stalling procedures. We were just trying to buy time, and the chances of cure were now few.

And yet, Anne was the most composed of us all. "When can we start, and how often do we need to do this?" she asked.

"We will start tomorrow. The drug is given subcutaneously, under the skin. It is given as two separate injections, with one in the abdomen and the other in the thigh. There are reports of it causing nausea, so we'll be sure to give medication to prevent that. You will need to come every day this week. We will continue watching your blood count on a weekly basis. I don't think you'll have to worry about side effects," I replied.

"Will it work?" Anne asked directly.

"I am hoping so. I really don't know. We have very limited experience in using this drug for post-remission relapses. The best we can hope for at this point is that the drug helps us achieve a stable disease until we can find a bone marrow transplant match. Time is the most valuable thing right now."

"Ahhh, there you are wrong, Dr. Patel, and I can correct you. Time is not the most valuable thing right now. It is the will of God that is most valuable. Whatever he decides will happen. I am ready for whatever is next, be it a healthy life or my final journey," Anne said.

To say that I was in awe would be an understatement. Words could not honestly express the marvel I felt when I heard Anne's words. I had never seen a patient who had become this adjusted to what would be the most uncertain part of their life. I had seen patients despair, cry, and become angry; I had never seen one this accepting and peaceful. It was always my job to reassure my patients. And yet Anne was doing just the opposite. It was as if I had come face-to-face with an enlightened soul whose understanding of life, death, and the journey it entails was complete. It almost felt as if I were listening to an angel.

# CHAPTER 9

# THE NEXT CHAPTER: JUST BEFORE THE END

*Living one day at a time;*

*Enjoying one moment at a time;*

*Accepting the hardship as a pathway to peace.*

*Taking, as He did, this sinful world*

*As it is, not as I would have it;*

*Trusting that He will make all things*

*If I surrender to His will;*

*That I may be reasonably happy in this life,*

*And supremely happy with Him forever in the next.*

—REINHOLD NIEBUHR

THE NEXT DAY, ANNE ARRIVED early in the morning to start her treatment. It went ahead without any hitches. She felt neither sick nor nauseous. The only issue was that her dropping blood count left her feeling weaker by the day. She felt out of breath even after walking a few yards. Telltale red spots had started appearing on her body. An arrangement was made for her to get red cell transfusions to help steady her breathing, make her feel better, and also improve her quality of life. Seven days of treatment went by without any major physical changes. Mental changes were a different matter, however. Anne seemed less and less interested in her day-to-day activities. Her time was now spent almost exclusively in prayer and worship. She resigned from social and volunteer commitments. She accepted that she was slowly drifting toward her final journey and destination of her heavenly abode. She could feel the Lord's presence all around her. While Dr. Spitzer, Connie, Shelton, and I were running around, desperately trying to artificially create a miracle, Anne seemed resigned to the fact that she was headed toward her home in glory.

Her blood count had stabilized for two weeks after starting the 5-azacytidine. The first part of our miracle had been sustained. Another bone marrow test was carried out. Praise God, it still reported no leukemia--so far, so good.

Anne had already completed two cycles of 5-azacytidine in a desperate attempt to halt the relentless progression of her myelodysplasia to acute leukemia. But after the first brief pause, our miracle gave way. Her blood count began dropping. Even after two more successive treatments, her count continued to worsen at a rapid pace. I was out of the country for the first weeks of January 2006 when Anne completed her two cycles of treatment and had another bone marrow test. It was all for naught. Her bone marrow revealed a full-blown leukemia. A conference call between Dr. Spitzer, my partner Dr. Gor, who was standing in my stead, and Dr. Khouri, a specialist from Emory Hospital in Atlanta, ended with the conclusion that 5-azacytidine had failed to arrest progression towards leukemia. Presently, Anne had full-blown leukemia. This time around was worse than before. Not only did it involve all cell lines, it also required her to have blood and platelet transfusions every other day. In late January, Dr. Spitzer finally decided to bite the bullet and move on with what was our last hope: a full-blown chemotherapy attack. We would throw everything we could at it, hoping that the massive doses of poisons would eliminate the monster that was raging in her blood long enough to try for a MUD bone marrow transplant. Only if the existing leukemia could be controlled would she be considered a suitable candidate for transplantation from an unrelated donor.

In the last week of January, Anne was asked to come to St. Francis Hospital once again. This time she would either make it through to fight another day or die trying. Although this fact was very obvious to all the medical personnel involved in her care, her family was still looking for a faint ray of hope, trying to grasp anything they could. It was true that patients had recovered from this stage in the past, but it was woefully and incredibly rare. Those patients were counted as miracles, and only God's miracle would save Anne now.

In a desperate attempt to salvage her body and bone marrow from progressive invasion and destruction by the leukemia, Dr. Spitzer decided on a salvage regimen for Anne. She was readmitted to St. Francis Hospital. She was now so weak from anemia that walking was nearly impossible. One by one her organ systems had started to be affected. Her breathing had become laborious partly from infection, as she had had no functioning immune system, and partly from the clogging of circulation in her lung blood vessels due to large leukemia cells lodging themselves in between blood vessels in the lungs.

It was almost a year since she was initially diagnosed with the horrible disease, and she had run the gamut of despair, treatment, hope, and finally, acceptance. She had been through all forms of suffering: living through chemotherapy, bone marrow transplantation, and traveling back and forth from doctors' offices and hospitals. And yet, it only led her closer and closer to death. She was worse today than the first day she walked into my office.

Much to my dismay, it was as if Anne knew this was the last lap of her life's journey. No one in her family understood what was coming her way, and she did not want to disappoint them by expressing what she was expecting.

Anne was admitted to that same room with the garden view. But this time, she detected a change in the attitude of the staff. The same nurses who once seemed jovial and full of joy when addressing her now had looks of pity on their faces whenever they walked into the room. This time, her hospitalization defied her previous familiarity, and she had a strange feeling of detachment. Everything had changed: her approach to life, her attitude about life, and her relationship with the world. She was a traveler on the last leg of her journey on this planet. All she wanted was some time to allow her family to heal and accept whatever outcome was barreling her way.

Anne received intensive chemotherapy to control her leukemia in hopes that she could enter a second remission. It didn't matter how short it was; it just had to be long enough for them to get a MUD transplant finished.

In football, sometimes a team is in a desperate situation. There are just twelve seconds left on the clock, there are no timeouts left, there are seventy or eighty yards to go, and a touchdown is needed for victory. In these situations, quarterbacks will do what is known as a Hail Mary pass. The quarterback says a Hail Mary prayer, the players line up, and everyone runs as fast as they can towards the end zone while the quarterback throws the ball as hard as he can, praying for a miracle. It works maybe once every hundred times it is attempted. It is an act of faith used when rationality dictates there is nothing that can be done. This last dose of chemo was our Hail Mary. Logic and experience told us that the fight was over, but we said our prayers, trusted our faith, and threw the ball as hard as we could anyway. We could only hope that someone caught it. This treatment plan was all that our All-Star team of oncologists could come up with. Make no mistake; we were aware that this was our last and most desperate attempt to fight off destiny.

No matter what we doctors believed, Anne was well aware that nothing was going to save her at this point. The only reason she tolerated the harsh and desperate therapy was for the sake of her family. While she had accepted that she would soon be facing her destiny at God's side, Shelton and Connie still had not. She didn't want them living with the guilt that they didn't do everything possible to try and save her.

With each passing day, Anne got weaker and weaker. Leukemic cells were invading every single one of her organs despite the continual chemo bombardment. She finished her chemotherapy on Valentine's Day. It was exactly one year since she was originally diagnosed.

Rather than experiencing improvements, her condition was progressively worsening. Now she needed a blood and platelet transfusion every week. Her lungs were covered with angry leukemic cells. In between the infections from the demolished immune system and lung blood vessels clogged with leukemia cells, doctors could no longer tell what was stopping her breathing. Many different specialists examined her, and each had a different opinion. But they all still had one thing in common. They established that her leukemia had become fastidious and was growing rapidly each day. Even a transplant by the world's best doctors in the world's best hospital wouldn't stop the relentless march of the leukemic blasts now. Everyone, however, from doctors to nurses, to Anne's family, to Anne herself, wanted one answer. What happened? What went wrong with her leukemia? Why did it return with such a vengeance? How did it avoid the deadly poisons unleashed by Dr. Spitzer and me? The answer would come soon.

I was not in the country when Anne's condition suddenly fell apart. I was in India visiting my parents with my wife and son. I didn't know about the drastic change in her health until I came back to the US. The last time I saw her was just before Christmas, and although I wasn't putting too much faith in the Vidaza treatment, I thought she had a reasonable chance of getting a MUD transplant. But when I came back in late January, Dr. Gor informed me of the situation. Although I was not directly involved in her care at St. Francis, I drove down to see her anyway. I had heard that she was struggling for her very life now. I contacted Dr. Creagh, a family friend of Anne and Shelton's who was also in Rock Hill. Both of us made the two-hour drive to Greenville to try to see if we could help her in any way. Nature seemed to have sensed our melancholy. The entire road was covered by torrents of freezing rain. The rain was so bad that it was impossible to see more than a few feet in front of the car. With a heavy heart, I realized that I was feeling the same way about the future course of Anne's life.

We eventually reached St. Francis Hospital and were taken to Anne's room—the same one she had always been in. She wasn't there when we arrived; they had taken her down to radiology for a test on her lungs. They were concerned that her breathing problems stemmed from a condition called ARDS (adult respiratory distress syndrome), a condition responsible for many deaths in hospital wards. When we arrived, the nurses told us that Anne was confused and sounded slightly senile in her speech patterns. This surprised me; Anne had always been exceptionally eloquent and good at communicating. Something was amiss. Another doctor came by and explained that it seemed a layer of inflammation made normal oxygen delivery difficult for Anne, and that her brain was slowly being deprived of oxygen, resulting in confusion and irrational behavior.

Shelton was waiting in the room. Connie had accompanied her mother downstairs. We sat down with him. The situation had hit him hard. It seemed as if wrinkles that normally take years to form had appeared on his face overnight. The bags under his eyes conveyed the long vigils he had spent by his wife's bedside. Seeing the changes in him almost broke my heart. Gary joined us, and we gently began a discussion about the end of life issues. ARDS carried a very high mortality rate and would cause many painful complications. We discussed whether or not Anne should be placed on a breathing machine, particularly considering the sudden changes in her behavior. After a long discussion with him, we decided that it might not be in her best interest. It wouldn't change the outcome. Since her leukemia had relentlessly progressed, there was no chance at a MUD transplant. Anne's condition was worsening on an exponential basis, her prognosis was poor, and there was no response to treatment so far. As her doctors, we decided, and Shelton agreed, not to place her on a breathing machine at the moment. We resolved to wait and see if the breathing problems were caused by leukemia or by ARDS. If it was ARDS, we would give her antibiotics, allowing her one more increasingly slim chance for at least a few more days.

Anne was brought back to the room. She had a broad smile, one that was shared by Connie. I couldn't quite believe my eyes. I was expecting to see her head slumped down, an oxygen mask over her face, and a confused expression reflected in her eyes. Instead, here she was, laboring through each breath but never losing her smile.

It turned out that earlier in the morning when Anne was taken down for a test, her oxygen cylinder didn't have enough oxygen. The confusion and disorientation was because she was breathing from a cylinder that had almost no oxygen left. It would have placed even a healthy person into delirium. We breathed a collective sigh of relief. At least there would be no breathing machine. We had dodged a bullet.

Seeing her alert and responsive felt like a miracle. I turned to look at Dr. Creagh and saw that he shared my wonder. We both honestly believed that we had come to Anne's deathbed when the nurses told us about the delirium.

We three doctors, Shelton, and Connie stood around Anne's bed. We all held each other's hands as Shelton began a prayer that we all repeated. He prayed for her as well as for each of us to help her, but more so to help her accept whatever the ultimate outcome was. The family knew that the sovereign will of God would prevail.

Although I was happy to see her recover from the brief episode of hypoxia, the look on her face, her feeble voice, and her body slowly wasting away all pointed towards her readiness to exit this form of existence for the afterlife.

Anne's condition was worsening day by day. Even Dr. Khouri, who was heading the effort for a MUD transplant, was losing hope. One of the major prerequisites for unrelated donor transplant was for Anne to be in remission. Her leukemia wasn't responding to our treatments, let alone considered to be in remission.

Dr. Spitzer decided to try to wrangle up a miracle. He did one more bone marrow test on Anne that would help make a final decision. Too many weeks had gone by without direction. It was obvious that Anne was aware her days remaining on earth could now be counted. Yet she had little control over what was happening, which disturbed her. She was glad that Dr. Spitzer was going to do the test. It was carried out on March 1.

The miracle we all hoped for didn't materialize. He walked slowly into her room with his face down and lacking his usual

Australian joviality. The look on his face told everyone all they needed to know. But they still had to have the discussion on what came next so they could make a fully informed decision.

Dr. Spitzer began, "The news isn't good. Almost ninety percent of the marrow space has been replaced with cancer cells. There is no space left for normal marrow maturation. I wish I could give you some hope, but at this point I think being completely honest is the best option. I honestly don't believe you will make it for more than a few weeks; if we're lucky, then maybe a month from now. I think the best thing is to consider what you want, rather than think about what we want for you."

As he spoke, he had none of his usual enthusiasm with him. Anne had touched the heart of everyone she came in contact with, including the grizzled old oncologist. He was extremely sorry that he had to deliver such sad news.

"You mean it's over? No, it can't be so! There must be some hope. There must be some procedure or hospital that can save her! Please don't say that she's going to die!" Connie burst out.

"I wish I had something different to tell you. I'm afraid that at some point we all are going to die of one thing or another. If there were any place that we could have sent her, neither Kashyap nor I would have hesitated for a second. But at this point, it's too late for even miracles. At this point, the best thing to do is to treasure every second that we still have with Anne, and we do whatever she wishes for her last days. Do not waste one single minute that can be shared." Gary was usually not one for talking like a philosopher; the family realized his seriousness.

"Can you at least tell us one thing? What happened? What went wrong with the leukemia?" Connie managed to ask in between tears. This was a question shared by everyone whose cancer suddenly stopped responding to chemo drugs.

"Leukemic cells are very intelligent. Anne's last bone marrow shows multiple new mutations, indicating that her leukemia cells have evolved into a much more aggressive form that is also very resistant and fastidious. They have developed MDR, multiple drug resistance genes. We still don't know exactly how it works or how to prevent it, but it causes these cells to become immune to the chemo poisons that destroyed them in the past. Scientists are still working diligently to try to prevent these genes from forming, but we are still miles away from a solution," Dr. Spitzer said.

His answer finally told us what had happened with Anne. Somewhere, some leukemia cells had survived the chemotherapy bombardment. These survivors developed a mutation that made them more aggressive and also resistant to chemotherapy. That was why none of our regimes worked any more and also why we couldn't get her into a second remission for the MUD transplant.

Anne then quietly asked, "Can I go home today? And if so, could I go now?" This was the first time Anne had intervened during the entire discussion.

She continued, "I want to spend my last few days in my own home, where I have spent the last two decades. I have fought a good fight, and I have known for the past few months that my time is coming to an end. I have no regrets."

"Yes, of course, Anne," Dr. Spitzer replied. "Let me coordinate all the arrangements for hospice care for you at home. I will have them send a nurse to your home to help ensure you are comfortable."

Dr. Spitzer started making arrangements immediately. He didn't want Anne to lose a single minute—nay, a single second—of the time she had left.

# CHAPTER 10

# THE FINAL PASSAGE

*O the deep, deep love of Jesus! vast, unmeasured, boundless , free,*
*Rolling as a mighty ocean in its fullness over me.*
*Underneath me, all around me, is the current of Your love;*
*Leading onward, leading homeward, to my glorious rest above.*
　—SAMUEL T. FRANCIS

Anne came home on March 2. She was not sure if her journey was ending or beginning. It was probably a mixture of both. Despite having a difficult time breathing and retaining oxygen, Anne's mind was very sharp and clear. As everyone else was busy preparing for the commencement of her final journey, Anne herself was at peace with her condition. She never resisted the idea of dying and leaving this world; she knew quite well that she would be going to her Heavenly Father.

Winter, spring, summer, fall, and then winter once more had passed since her first diagnosis. Last winter, the family was hoping for a cure for Anne. This winter, the family was hoping for as many weeks as God was willing to grant them with one of his earthly angels. Anne had become very weak and fragile. She had lost a lot of weight. Her body's normal tissues were losing the battle against the immortal and ever-replicating leukemia cells. Day by day and inch by inch, her body was slowly dying, one bit of tissue at a time. Remarkably, no matter how much havoc leukemia wreaked on Anne's physical body, it was not able to break her will and faith in her Lord and Savior Jesus Christ. No matter what Anne had to endure at the end, she would be the victor. Neither the fear of bodily suffering nor the apprehension of physical death was able to take away the wonderful and illustrious smile that her weak and wrinkled face couldn't hide. She was currently witnessing God's grace everywhere. Even in her own suffering, she saw the Lord's hand at work and believed that he would bring about his perfect will for his glory.

Anne's suffering in the last few days had been increasingly obvious. Her face was pale and colorless, and simply walking a few steps turned into a strenuous exercise. Anne's bed was placed against the wall facing her backyard so that she could enjoy the beauty of nature in comfort. She especially loved looking at her daffodils that were beginning to bloom in the yard. Her frailty no longer allowed her to stand on the deck.

Even in the harshness of winter, a backyard that was dry, barren, and filled with leafless trees couldn't shake her belief in the Lord's care for all things. She still saw the occasional squirrel run around the dry branches, and a bird that must have been lost somewhere en route to Florida made its home there. These sights reminded her of God's presence. He had granted life to a bird where logi- cally there should have been none. Its voice reminded her of the voice of the Creator that she now heard everywhere. As night fell, she could see faint lights from distant stars, barely gleaming, overshadowed by bright city lights. This reminded her that the Almighty God's presence spanned across many galaxies, reaching millions of light years away.

On March 3, I decided to pay a home visit to see how Anne was doing and if I could help ease her pain in any way. Although she had been enfeebled, Anne was still fully able to compose words and express herself in a clear fashion.

"Anne, how are you feeling today?" I began as softly and gently as I could.

She smiled up at me and said, "Bodily, you can see I am quite weak and fragile, Dr. Patel. But mentally, I'm still the same woman I've always been! If anything, now I'm finally at ease and comfortable with the direction God has decided to take me. I think he wants me by his side sooner rather than later! At least I'm no longer confused about how much longer I have!"

"Are you in any discomfort? Do you hurt at all?" I was trying to discover if there were any symptoms that I could help her with. "Please don't hesitate to ask for any pain medicines. It's okay to ask for help. I know that time is limited. As much as I wish that you could stay with us, I think it is evident from our losing battle against the leukemia that the Lord has different plans for you. If he wills, you shall soon see your Savior Jesus Christ face to face."

"Do you really believe so, Dr. Patel?" Anne asked.

"Yes, Anne, I do believe that once you leave this physical body, you will be moving to a heavenly abode and the presence of the Lord," I replied.

"I believe so too," Anne reaffirmed her faith. "What do you believe about death based on your faith?"

"I'm sure you recall our conversations before. My belief system is a mix of Hinduism, Christianity, Judaism, Buddhism, and Islam, only further compounded and complicated by my own research and experiences as a scientist. What I consider to be most important is this:

We all are children of God.

We all are born at his order and mercy.

Upon death, we return the temporary body that we borrowed to the five elements–

earth, water, fire, space, and air–for the purpose of recycling so that new life forms will not run short of the raw material that is needed.

The spirit or the soul within the body, which is also the divine element called the life force by some, abides within all of us and will find its way back to the Almighty.

We will come back to exist in whatever life form that he ordains."

So speaking, I elaborated on my own concept of life, death, and the afterlife.

"You sound like a philosopher. Do you believe in reincarnation, Dr. Patel?" Although bodily very weak and fragile, Anne had a very strong presence of mind and had retained her composure and faith unabatedly.

"Yes and no. At the risk of sounding like a noncommittal politician, I'll admit my beliefs change based on what I see. I am constantly listening to my inner voice and coming up with the answers.

"I believe that we are given an opportunity in this lifetime to witness the Almighty everywhere and in all his glory. Our body represents a combination of the basic recyclable elements that we identify a person with. Deeper within our conscience and beyond the reaches of untrained minds is the soul, or the life force, that represents divinity within. For sacred souls like you, this lifetime journey will take you back to the Almighty's kingdom. To this extent I believe in rebirth for the explicit purpose of achieving the union with the Almighty. If I may say so, I think that you have achieved it, Anne. In these last few months, each meeting with you has convinced me more and more that you are not an earthly being but rather an angel, a messenger in disguise. It is no wonder that God wants you with him soon."

I took a break and then continued.

"For an icicle from winter storm, warmth from sun ends its life.

We call that life water.

For that water drop that drains into a stream, life ends as a raindrop.

We call that new life stream.

As stream merges into river, it ceases to exist as stream and re-incarnates itself as river.

When river ends in an ocean, its existence as a river ends; there-after that same raindrop ends, only to be known as a part of vast, infinite, and eternal ocean.

When ocean warms up, water vapor rises and metamorphoses itself as a cloud, life as a part of ocean water ceases, and new physi-cal life begins in sky.

In winter storm, that water drop falls from sky, dying as a cloud form only to become an icicle.

Icicle again moves down as water, dew drop, or raindrop that never makes it back to the ocean.

This raindrop will rise again when destined."

I concluded my thoughts.

"Our lives are like the life cycle of this icicle or raindrop.

At times it is stream.

Another time it is river, and then sometimes it will go deep as a mighty ocean."

I finished there.

Anne maintained her solid belief that Jesus Christ had secured eternal salvation for her through his sacrificial death on the cross.

She knew that throughout her earthly journey he was with her and he loved her. She accepted that leukemia was part of God's sovereign will for her life. She had no regrets and was ready for the Lord to come and take her to her heavenly home.

As she spoke to me, her voice grew more feeble. The effects of her most recent morphine dose were making themselves known, and Anne's speed of talking had slowed near the end of our conversation.

"Can I be of any help in making this transition between this life and what comes after, Anne?" I was torn between my personal attachment to her and a desire to allow her as much time as possible in privacy with her family.

"Oh, Dr. Patel, you have truly been a godsend. You have made this journey so much easier for my family and me to weather. You've done all you can for me now. May God bless you! My desire is to see you someday in the kingdom of heaven with our Holy Father."

Those were Anne's final words to me.

I couldn't speak at all; my voice was choked with tears. I said my last goodbye to the lady who had so touched the most inner part of my soul.

The hours went quickly thereafter. Although Anne was getting weaker physically, her spirit had somehow become somewhat restless. Her eyes, often vacant, were staring at the sky outside the window almost all the time now. It was as if she was seeing something the others couldn't. She was straining her ears and spoke of heavenly music the others couldn't hear.

Finally, it was Shelton who realized what was happening. Her pastor husband, long-time lover, and true philanthropist was able to connect the dots.

Shelton realized that Anne was looking for permission to begin her journey to heaven. He asked all the family members, including her daughters, sons-in-law, son, grandchildren, and the dog to come in her room.

Anne's family held hands as her husband began to pray.

He then slowly touched her hand, took it into his own, kissed her on her cheek, and said, "Anne, I love you. I know you can't wait to go to be with Jesus in heaven. I can't begin to say how grateful I am for your love and companionship throughout my life. You have been my light and my joy for so many years. You were by my side in rough and gentle times. There are countless reasons for me to want to say 'please don't leave me here by myself.' But I think that I need not be selfish now. There is just one reason to say that you have my permission to move on. The reason is that I know you are going to Jesus, our Savior. You will be in God's presence, and that reason trumps all that I can offer. I love you, sweetheart. All of us love you with all our hearts. Your death will leave a permanent hole in our hearts. We are going to miss you so much, my love. But whenever you are ready, it is okay for you to move on. I will miss you always, until we are reunited in God's heavenly kingdom. I can't wait to join you and behold the glory and beauty of our Lord Jesus."

One after the other, all the family members came to give Anne their goodbyes. As hard as it was to do, they were at least thankful that the Lord had allowed them the time and opportunity to do so. Even the family dog came and sat silently by her side, maintaining a quiet vigil.

Shelton's words made a monumental difference. After everyone had said goodbye, Anne appeared very relaxed. Her vacant eyes were no longer searching the sky. Her breathing slowed down. She looked extremely comfortable and was totally quiet. For the next day, Anne slept most of the time. She did not appear to be in any pain or discomfort at all. Shelton thought of the times too numerous to count where he had been part of a family's bedside vigil. He had prayed, loved, and encouraged. But he truly had never realized the great depths of pain those last moments held for loved ones. He had thought he knew. It surprised him to realize how very fragile he actually was in those moments. His eyes filled with tears, and his heart filled with grief. It was Anne, on the other hand, who was serenely composed. She had accepted the realities of life and death.

Two days later, on the evening of March 7, Shelton and Lucy were both sitting beside Anne's bed. The dog was sleeping on the floor, and Connie, Palmer, and the grandchildren were in another room. Her breathing was heavier and deeper than usual. She was slowly slipping into a coma. She was already on intravenous morphine injections to prevent any anxiety or stress from pain, since she no longer had the ability to express herself. Suddenly, they both saw Anne's face brighten up, as if she had glimpsed something heading her way. It was as if she had just witnessed Jesus coming down for her as he said he would in John 14. "I go to prepare a place for you, and I will come again and receive you unto myself." She stirred and opened her eyes wide. Lucy called for Connie and Palmer to come quickly. The grandchildren also came to the room. She slightly lifted her head towards the ceiling. She looked around and raised her hands in the air—a look of tranquil peace and calm shone on her face. It was as if Jesus was reaching down to her, and she was trying to take his hand. Shelton helped her lift her back up, fully aware that the time had arrived for Anne to depart from this world. Though he couldn't see anything, he felt the presence of Jesus in the room. He felt something slip off his hands and slowly, gently drift towards heaven. Despite his grief, he felt in total and complete awe. The movement was so smooth, so elegant, that he had no words to describe it. It was felt and yet never felt. Was he witnessing a miracle? Anne opened her mouth and made one final smile.

Anne's body felt a little bit lighter. With her eyes still radiating sparkling love and affection, Shelton hugged her. Those last few seconds felt like an eternity to him. In Anne's body, he was witnessing the power of the Lord's love firsthand. He could sense the warmth and the brightness of his glory. He was so engrossed in the majestic and divine moment that he felt like he was frozen in time and that he would be in this embrace with his loved one for eternity.

Suddenly he felt a jerk, followed by a heavy feeling on his hands.

The life had finally crept out of Anne's body. At that very instant, her soul was with the angels, rising to the side of the Lord, leaving the lifeless shell behind in the hands of her loved one. The bright light had vanished for Shelton, both literally and figuratively. The warmth and humidity of eternal ocean had disappeared. Tears rolled down his cheeks. Everyone felt the sudden change in the room. Life as they had known it had changed forever. The whole family fell into grief.

Within the next few days, Anne's physical body underwent burial. The spirit that had graced and brightened the lives of so many, including myself, had left the earth and moved on to heaven. She left behind not just a physical body and a grave, but an imprint on the hearts of everyone she came into contact with. Churchgoers, fellow volunteers, nurses, MOA's, doctors, and family alike grieved. During the visitation, everyone in the room remembered Anne's deep love for people and her absolute assurance in the promises of God.

Anne's greatest desire during her time of suffering and death was to be a faithful witness to her Lord and Savior Jesus Christ. From the day after her diagnosis, she claimed Isaiah 43:10 to be her life verse. If you visit her grave in Laurelwood Cemetery in Rock Hill, you will find engraved on her burial marker these words: "You are My witnesses, declares the Lord, and My servant whom I have chosen" (Isaiah 43:10).

Her memorial service at Westminster Presbyterian Church following her death was glorious and Christ-centered. As was her manner of life, she made it clear that it was not about her but about her Lord Jesus who had loved her, saved her, and taken her to glory.

It may take years for me to fully understand the depths of Anne's influence on my life and profession. I will simply put voice to truth–in her own joyful way, Anne changed me. Not many people can say that they have spoken to, hugged, and felt the touch of an angel. But after the year I spent with Anne Sanford, I can say that I did.

Anne's unwavering faith had such a profound effect on me that I decided to learn more about Christianity and in a much deeper way. This ultimately led me and my wife to visit the Holy Land. We also invited a retired pastor to carry out Bible studies at our office every Friday afternoon.

In full assurance of faith, I do willingly accept Jesus Christ, the Son of God, as the only hope for salvation. As Anne believed, I now believe. I have witnessed and experienced continued blessings from my Precious Savior in allowing me to carry on my work faithfully and altruistically.

Anne's story is one of encouragement and hope in the midst of suffering. She was a faithful witness of Jesus Christ. At her memorial service, the testimony of her life was compared to the Apostle

Paul in II Timothy 4:7–8. "I have fought the good fight, I have finished the race, I have kept the faith. Henceforth, there is laid up for me the crown of righteousness, which the Lord, the righteous Judge, will award me on that day, and not only to me, but to all who have loved his appearing."